THE 144 'DOORS' OF THE ZODIAC: THE DWAD TECHNIQUE

by
Thyrza Escobar

First Printing 1974
Revised 1986
ISBN Number: 0-86690-314-3
Library of Congress Catalog Card Number: 85-73312

Cover Design: Lynda Kay Fullerton

Published by:
American Federation of Astrologers, Inc.
P.O. Box 22040, 6535 South Rural Road
Tempe, Arizona 85282

Printed in the United States of America

Gratefully dedicated
to the Memory of
Carl Leipert

TABLE OF CONTENTS

LIST OF FIGURES

LIST OF TABLES

FOREWORD

The first edition of *The 144 'Doors'* — *The Dwad Technique* was published in 1974 as part of a volume which included Ephemerides, calculated by J. Allen Jones, of Lilith and Lulu as well as of the True Nodes of the Moon and Planets. That edition has long been out-of-print.

This new edition of the *144 'Doors'* is revised and enlarged. The order of some of the original material has been changed to bring continuity with the inclusion of material that was omitted in the 1974 edition.

If a beginning student, you will find the Astro-Vocabulary of Key-words and Phrases a sound foundation for this symbolic language that is Astrology.

If an advanced student, this portion of the book will be, I hope, a review which gives Carl Leipert's use of Key-words in a basic vocabulary of the language of Astrology. His Key-words and phrases were in German, his native language.

I did not speak German at all. His English was very fluent although heavily accented. He said his skill with written English was inadequate for writing texts, that I should carry on his work in English. When I questioned him in early 1936 why he did not write in German, he answered that it would 'all be lost' if written in German! "Something would happen to it," he stated. Although he stated that there were in 1936 and would be outstanding astrological texts in German — his own (if he wrote them then) would be lost.

From a College Dictionary in English I carefully made lists of words appropriate, in my opinion, for Planets, Signs, Houses, Aspects, etc. which I submitted to him for his approval. These are the Key-words I have used ever since.

Do not try to memorize this Basic Astro-Vocabulary. They now begin this book, so placed for easy reference. Do not feel confined by them; I use many others as well. But these suggest other Key-words of similar meanings.

This edition retains the material on Divisions of the Zodiacal Circle, + (positive) and − (negative) areas. Decanates are given to provide a background or coloring in their areas. Added, in Appendix I, is an easy method to find the Chaldean rulers of the Decans without a Table for reference.

I am so pleased to add the material on the Longitudinal Parallels as Leipert called them.

In my years of study before Leipert became my teacher (mentor is a better word), I had used the Antiscia as they were generally called and had no realization of their tremendous value. Leipert interpreted them by the Dwads occupied. They added a new dimension.

From the very first the use of the Dwads was amazingly effective. But the Dwads relative to these Longitudinal Parallels, whether in the Natal or activated Potential were almost incredible when "specifics and particulars" were verified by analysands. They provide subtle but powerful contacts between Planets that, without them, might appear to be unrelated.

Leipert considered the Universal Language of Astrology to involve Science, Psychology, Philosophy, Religion and Art. Science, as its mathematical calculations, astronomical measurements and placements, its anatomy, so to speak, and the centuries of observed correlation of celestial phenomena with events on Earth. Psychology, as science of the Psyche. Leipert was an earnest and devoted student of Jungian Analytical Psychology. Philosophy, as the love of wisdom; the Way. Religion, as the linking back to Source, in harmony with all the great scriptures of the ages. (He had made a deep study of Comparative Religion as well as the Judaic — Christian teachings and was well versed in Qabalah, the oral tradition.) Art, as the interpretive side.

Analysis and synthesis of the Natal Charts and cycles should be a creative experience for both the astrologer and the analysand. It should be revealing and constructive to be worthwhile. If not constructive, the interpretation is not a true interpretation, because then it would fall short of the Art of interpretation.

Leipert's interpretations were metaphysical in that he included the phenomenal world of physical body, environment, people, places and things shown by the Radix. But he included the psychological with the physical and the spiritual with the material.

I acknowledge my lasting gratitude to Carl Leipert. Without his many "clues" and "leads" this book would not have been written.

I am so grateful to J. Allen Jones for his dependable and generous help. He contributed all the Tables of Dwads for Solar Eclipses and Major Conjunctions. I have used his Ephemeris of Lilith, Lulu and the True Nodes of Moon and Planets. Without his help in these items and his tireless typing, this new edition might not have been made.

I heartily thank my friend and protegee, Karen Allen, for her graciously relieving me of some of my astrological practice with clients who are in Jungian analysis. Because of her I had the time to prepare this new and enlarged edition of *144 'Doors'*.

And I thank Sara Cooper of the A.F.A. for her expertise and caring in doing all the Figures.

Do you realize that more than a hundred years of study and research are in the background of this book? I began to study Astrology by myself in Ohio in Jan. 1922. Since summer 1923, in California, I have set up and analysed thousands of Natal Charts. Since private study with Leipert (Feb. 1936 through July 1938) I have used his "clues," hints and suggestions and leads in my analyses. He had studied and researched for more than 40 years. So, altogether, more than a century of study and observation is in the background of this book. I hope you, too, will continue on and on!

Sincerely

Thyrza Escobar

Covina, California

Spring 1984

ASTRO VOCABULARY

Let us acquire a basic vocabulary of Key-words and Key-phrases for the Sun, Moon and Planets.

Basic Key-words and Key-phrases for Natal Planets

The Sun, really a Star, and the Moon, a Satellite of Earth, will be classified with the Planets for the sake of convenience. The Sun and Moon are frequently referred to as "the Lights." It does save space to include them with Natal *Planets*. "*Natal* Planets" = planetary positions in Celestial Longitude at the time of the birth of a person.

☉ The SUN: the ego, center of consciousness, sense of identity, "I-amness" of the individual (whether or not so recognized by others), will, vitality, illumination, Masculine Principle, etc. The Sun rules the Sign Leo.

☽ The MOON: instincts, responses, moods, phases, fluctuations, receptivity, reflection, impressionability, the Feminine Principle, etc. The Moon rules Cancer.

The Sun stands for the Masculine Principle as it manifests through the person himself or herself or through the men in the life; the Moon stands, similarly, for the Feminine Principle as it manifests through the person himself or herself or through the women in the life.

☿ MERCURY: perception as such, particularly sensory perception, observation, attention, reason or rationalization, "the avenue of expression," communication (verbal or other), decisions, etc. Mercury rules Gemini and Virgo.

♀ VENUS: values, appreciation, beauty, attraction, arts, artistry, affection, cohesion, ease, etc. Venus rules Taurus and Libra.

♂ MARS: initiative, desire, exertion, energy in action, on the offense or on the defense, construction or destruction, advance or retreat, etc. Mars rules Aries and Scorpio.

Note the interesting contrasts between Venus and Mars: Mars shows how you go forth into action, the beginning, efforts made, etc.; Venus indicates the finishing touches, finesse, the meaning and the fruit of experience.

♃ JUPITER: expansion, extension, compensation (in a psychological or other sense), future plans, religion and/or philosophy, breadth, etc. Jupiter rules Sagittarius and (with Neptune) co-rules Pisces. In the old days Jupiter alone was considered to be the sole Ruler of Pisces. However, after Neptune was discovered — in 1846 — it was given co-rulership of Pisces, along with Jupiter.

Let us note some contrasts between Mercury and Jupiter. Mercury shows the perception of the "outer" world by means of the senses, concrete information, etc. Jupiter is revelation, revelation of the Unconscious (often through dreams), and judgment which takes into consideration abstractions or invisible factors. Carl Leipert stated that Jupiter is the Natal Planet which particularly indicates the man's Anima and the woman's Animus (in a Jungian sense).

♄ SATURN: structure, framework, pattern, tradition, discipline, authority, crystallization, rigidity, caution, the time element, that which is old or long-term, and so on. Saturn rules Capricorn and, with Uranus (discovered in 1781) co-rules Aquarius.

♅ URANUS: newness or renewal, the unusual or the unexpected, distinctiveness, individualism, individuation, originality, uniqueness, design, innovation, the ultra modern and/or antiquities, inspiration, the human element, etc. Uranus is the co-ruler of Aquarius.

♆ NEPTUNE: imagery, fantasy, idealism, assumptions, obligations, the Unconscious, the unknown, sublety, that which is elusive, mystery, mysticism, belief, what is taken for granted, etc. Neptune is now said to co-rule Pisces.

♀ PLUTO: integration (in a psychological or sociological sense), organization or re-organization, complexity or possibly complications, groups, etc. Carl Leipert considered Pluto to indicate the *Collective* Unconscious.

There still continues to be a controversy about which Sign is co-ruled by Pluto. Although a large number of astrologers believe that Pluto co-rules Scorpio, many others do not accept this, taking Pluto to be co-ruler of Aries. I personally follow this Pluto co-rules *Aries* school of thought. Leipert said he was strongly "leaning" toward the Aries instead of Scorpio; but he did not live long enough for definite confirmation, of a thousand Charts for unquestionable confirmation.

I have listed the Planets in this order: the Lights (Sun and Moon), followed, in the order of their speeds of motion, by five Planets known by the ancients: Mercury, Venus, Mars, Jupiter, and Saturn; then the three more recently discovered ones: Uranus, Neptune, and Pluto, the three sometimes called the "higher-octave Planets." Uranus might be called the higher-octave of Mercury, Planet of observation and reason: Uranus is the flash of inspiration and insight. Neptune, compassion and sympathy, is the higher-octave of Venus, affection and fondness. With Pluto there is still some uncertainty; some consider it to be the higher-octave of Mars, Planet of own effort and personal action: Pluto shows mass production or collective, highly organized actions. The suggestion has been made, however, for Pluto, organized groups, to be the higher-octave of the Moon, the masses.

⊕ The EARTH: the physical, actual world of three dimensions, mundane matters, etc. Many astrologers, perhaps most astrologers, do not take the Planet Earth into consideration at all in the analysis of the Natal Planets. This was not true of Carl Leipert who always included the Earth in his interpretation.

The Natal Earth always occupies the Celestial Longitude directly opposite that of the Natal Sun. The Earth is not given in the *Ephemeris*; but you know its position from the Sun, exactly opposite.

In the calculated Radix Chart (the Map of Birth) the Earth is not marked in the Chart itself; the Earth is at the center. In fact, some horoscope blanks show a partial map of the world at the center. Leipert found that physical characteristics and particular features are often well shown by the Sign in which the Earth was at the time of birth.

Be sure to distinguish the glyph for the Earth, ⊕, from that for the Part of Fortuna (Fortuna) a so-called Arabian Part which is a sensitive point in the calculated Radix Chart, set up when the time and place of birth are known. Leipert suggested that for the Part of Fortune we use an "X" within a circle, ⊗, to distinguish it from the Planet Earth.

Leipert said the Earth probably shared with the Moon the rulership of the Sign Cancer. The Moon is a Satellite of the Earth. Moreover, "Mother Earth" is a significant figure in many of the legends throughout the world. Astrologically both the Moon and the Earth are very important in the indications about the mother.

⊗ FORTUNA (The Part of Fortune): because the calculation of the Part of Fortune (Fortuna) involves the Sun, Moon, and Radix Ascendant, it is a very significant Sensitive Point, located the same distance from the Asc. that the Moon is from the Sun. C. Aq. Libra called it the "Part of Happiness." Other Key-words: contentment, satisfaction, gratification.

Lilith

Back in 1932 came my introduction to Lilith by means of Sepharial's *The Science of Foreknowledge*. Lilith was not a stranger because of her appearance in legends. Sepharial made the astrological introduction. My, should I say, curiosity? Excited, I was eager to see where Lilith was in my growing collection of Charts of relatives and friends. But where was there an Ephemeris for Lilith? Sepharial listed enough information that I was able to work out an "Ephemeris" of a kind with approximate positions.

After about two years of noting Lilith's Transits and some study of Natal Lilith in my collection of Charts, it seemed time for me to share this information with the members of a class I was then teaching at the First Temple and College of Astrology in Los Angeles.

In a number of instances it did seem that Lilith (natally or by transit) was involved in venomous bites and stings as well as in food poisoning, infection, etc. Such conditions as these certainly did not always coincide, apparently, with Lilith; but they did coincide often enough to be interesting. At times Lilith seemed to indicate nightmares and dreams that were very strange, some very meaningful.

In 1936 Leipert and I exchanged what we had, respectively, noted about Lilith. He, too, had read Sepharial's book and had compiled a kind of "Ephemeris" similar to mine, adequate for obtaining approximate positions of Lilith.

His work with Lilith had convinced him of the correspondence of Lilith with certain meanings of the Shadow, in a Jungian sense. Leipert too had noted the dreams which had sometimes coincided with Transiting Lilith or with activation of the Natal Lilith in Charts. He had been far more impressed by the apparently psychological "impact" of Lilith than by the more physiological coincidences (bites, stings, poisonings, and so on). He did not deny the latter at times, but found the psychological correspondences much more outstanding.

If you are not familiar with Sepharial's material on Lilith, given in his book, *The Science of Foreknowledge,* this is, I feel, the time to refer to it.

Lilith is supposedly a satellite of the Earth, a moon that does not reflect the light from the Sun; so it is called a Dark Moon. The name "Lilith" is related to the Hebrew word for "night." Sepharial quoted Dr. Wynn Westcott, saying, "Lilith means a dust-cloud, but is also translated as Owl and as Screeching Bird of Night."

Sepharial himself named this Satellite "Lilith." What Satellite? If you ask about this Dark Satellite at the neighboring Planetarium, you might well be told Lilith does not exist at all. Then how did Sepharial become interested?

He listed a number of recorded observations of Earth Satellites (not those sent up in recent years). Some were recorded as a "round black body" seen as it crossed the Sun's disc. A Dr. Waldemath in Hamburg is credited with the discovery of this second Satellite of Earth with its publication made on January 22, 1898. His article in the *Globe,* dated February 7, 1898, (according to Sepharial) mentioned various observations of the Satellite, dates of its Transit across the Solar disc, etc. Its synodical revolution was given, based on the observed Transit.

Sepharial proposed the symbol ⊖, an "O" with a horizontal cross-bar, implying, to my way of thinking, a zero with a minus sign in it! It has not been "accepted" generally within astronomical circles, and, until recent years it was not of wide concern within astrological circles.

Sepharial gave instructions on how to determine the Longitude of Lilith according to the information given by Dr. Waldemath. This was the basis for Leipert's approximate Ephemeris as well as my sketchy one.

Sepharial's suggestions about the interpretation of Lilith (which I find somewhat too one-sided) are: "obstructive and fatal, productive of various forms of catastrophes and accidents, sudden upsets, changes, and states of confusion" (page 51). In addition, "rapid changes and upsets, . . . unfortunate and violent, disruptive and fatal" (page 53). Remember, these are quotations from Sepharial.

Lilith and Lulu

Sepharial included a few examples of Lilith in Charts, citing what he had attributed to Lilith in the way of events. He emphasizes "danger."

In *Raphael's Ephemeris for 1935* a page is devoted to Lilith and Lulu, with emphasis on Lilith. Raphael stated he had read Sepharial's book as early as 1919. He continued: "The thoughtful student with a critical bent will naturally ask, how comes it that if these two orbs exist our wonderfully expert and super-equipped observatories have not spotted them? That is exactly the position that I cannot answer. For fifteen years the matter has been 'an open question' in my mind, yet constantly and frequently the practical results and evidence has been such as to provide the 'missing links' and to compel my *unwilling belief.*

"Of this 'Lilith' I could tell many curious stories — stories that might be hard to believe. Lilith has some relation to drastic poisons, drainage, sex force and seems destructive." . . . It is not without a curious striking interest that 'Sepharial', the great writer and exponent of this orb, should have been born with Lilith upon his meridian. . . . This remarkable author met his death in December, 1929, as a result of an epidemic of poisoned or contaminated milk."

Here again, we see this connection between Lilith and poisoning, which both Leipert and I had noted; neither of us, however, noted fatal cases of poisoning.

Raphael acknowleged he had received an *Ephemeris of the Two* "dark moons" compiled and published by W. van Breda Beausar, of Bandoeng. This *Ephemeris* of the two Dark Moons covered 1870 to 1936 inclusive, with Longitudes for the 1st of each month.

This *Ephemeris* to which Raphael referred adds some information from the noted Dutch astrologer, C. Aq. Libra (the pen name for the compiler of the *Ephemeris*).

C. Aq. Libra said Lilith appears to have its exaltation in Gemini. He stated Lilith "is not unlike Uranus" in nature; "two of its symbols are the owl and the monkey. It has a relation with birth." He used another symbol for Lilith, ⁺☽, a plus sign in front of the symbol for the Moon. Leipert used ∅.

Sepharial had referred to still another Dark Moon of the Earth with opinions — of Dr. Waltemath — regarding it. Sepharial did not give any specific name to this "Third Moon" of the Earth. However, C. Aq. Libra gave it the name "Lulu," and with this name, a symbol, °☽, a small circle in front of the symbol for the Moon. He said the Exaltation of Lulu appears to be in Leo. He said Lulu "is not unlike Neptune" in nature. "It has also a relation with birth and sex." He gave Lulu a "benefic" nature, and said Lulu's symbol is probably Eve.

It is significant that Lilith preceded Eve in some of the old legends.

Some years ago I asked J. Allen Jones to compute the Longitudes of both Dark Moons from the conjunctions with the Sun, instead of "running" them ahead the 63 years according to their period (because with the intervening leap years and the consequent "extra Day" at times, there is too much chance for error). Since not all the elements of their orbits are known, the Longitudes may have a deviation of approximately one degree (or less) for Lilith and less than half a degree for Lulu per day. Therefore, we should be able to place the Lilith within its correct Dwad or the adjacent one when its position is right on the "boundary" line between Dwads; then, when there is some doubt, you should note both possible — "tentative" Dwads with a question; probably observation of the correlations between the Dwads with Natal interpretation and verification by Transits over that point will determine which of the two possible Dwads is the correct one.

So many of the interpretations which I have heard and read have not conformed to either Leipert's or my own observation of conditions and events correlated with Lilith. Countless effective Transits of Lilith or effective Transits to the Natal Lilith have not been fatal! In many instances there were no indications whatsoever about poisonings, bites, stings, physical danger, etc. when such or similar conditions and events might have been expected, according to some of the sensationally dire interpretations of Lilith.

Granted, it is wise to use extra precautions about such things (and about allergies too) when Lilith is activated. It is no time to disregard matters when you are "in the dark" about them. This is a phrase very much used by Leipert when he interpreted Lilith. But he vehemently asserted that Lilith is not always indicative of that which is sinister and dangerous. It may be dangerous, but not always in a negative sense. We often fear what is in the dark, whether this is a reasonable fear or not. We don't know who or what might be there! At times the fear may be valid and highly protective; but it might not be valid at all, and just as paralyzing. The "darkness" referred to is more than actual darkness.

We should not forget that the "Darkness" may hold treasure as well as trash or opportunity as well as threat. There is much that is positive as well as the negative.

The times when the Transiting Sun conjoins the Natal Lilith and when the Transiting Lilith conjoins Natal Sun are especially indicative of times to bring light to the darkness. Pay extra attention to this; it is very significant.

Lilith represents (should we say, "personifies"?) in a manner no other Point or Planet in the Chart does to like extent, the abysmal, shadowy darkness. It is an important astrological component of the Shadow, in a Jungian sense, the Shadow we seem to encounter in the other person, which is also our own.

Often the Shadow correlates with characteristics (negative and positive), even with talents we did not know were ours. It is "what we are in the dark about."

Other activations of Lilith often bring this "in the darkness" to our attention and into our experience. But, as stated above, the Conjunctions between Lilith and the Sun are especially enlightening and meaningful.

The Key-words "Shadow, darkness, in the dark" are nearly always appropriate.

Natal Lilith is described and characterized by its Sign position; specifics and particulars indicated by the Dwad occupied. The Radix House occupied shows where, with whom and with what the Shadow is encountered most in actual experience, also in which department of life there tends to be some darkness in which is more than may ever come to light in a lifetime. From time to time, though, more light is cast there. Leipert used to say, "There you can follow the Shadow back to the substance."

Furthermore, he compared Lilith to the shading in a painting. "Without the shading there is not so much depth. A poster without any shading may be brilliant and effective; but it does not have the depth in it. The contrast between shadow and light gives an added dimension to the painting. So it is in the Chart: recognition of the Shadow seems to intensify the highlights."

Leipert for nearly 20 years used Lilith in his Charts, carefully noting his observed correlations. But he used Lulu for less than 5 years; he did not make any definite statements to me about Lulu. Personally, I feel we should note Lulu too; in time we should have some valid correlations, although I have not been impressed with Lulu, as I have been by the striking correlations with Lilith.

Both Lilith and Lulu, being Moons albeit Dark Moons, relate to moods, feelings, and responses. In a way they are similar to Luna, the Moon that reflects light. However, feelings and responses attributed to Lilith and Lulu are less clear, more "in the dark."

In Synastry, Lilith may show a kind of fascination that is indescribable. At times there may be such a sense of the unknown or of such depths of feeling that there is uneasiness of being "beyond one's depth."

In Synastry Lulu may be equally fascinating as Lilith, but without the sometimes fearsome feeling of being "beyond one's depth" in feeling. This, too, may indicate a feeling or response that is difficult to explain in ordinary ways.

I have found Lilith and Lulu very significant in both personal life and career fields. One, or both, may be very important for artists, painters, lighting or stage designers, photographers, etc. — those who deal with darkness and light literally. One or the other may be very significant in the charts of teachers, researchers, psychologists and others who deal with darkness and light in a figurative sense. You see, while the Sun equates with light and consciousness, Lilith and Lulu relate to the deep levels of the unconscious.

I use the glyph $\varnothing$ for Lilith and a $\rangle$ for Lulu (darkened to distinguish from $\mathbb{D}$ — Luna).

The Moon's Nodes

The *North* Node (also called the Ascending Node) is the point on the Ecliptic — the apparent path of the Sun — where the Moon crosses from South to North Celestial Latitude; at that point that Moon is said to be on its North Node.

The *South* Node (also called the Descending Node) is the point on the Ecliptic — the apparent path of the Sun — where the Moon crosses from North to South Celestial Latitude; there it is said to be on its South Node.

8

For more about the positions of the Nodes, please refer to the Ephemerides. Now we are interested in some appropriate Key-words and Key-phrases for the Nodes of the Moon.

☊ The Moon's *NORTH* NODE (often called the Dragon's Head): confidence, gain, etc.

☋ The Moon's *SOUTH* NODE (often called the Dragon's Tail): release (in a psychological or other sense), "letting go," that which is more or less automatic, etc.

The "mean" or average position of the Moon's North Node is listed in the *Ephemeris* for the year. Carl Leipert was insistent upon the use of the TRUE Nodes instead of the mean Nodes. Fortunately, J. Allen Jones has computed the True Nodes which are in *True Nodes of Moon and Planets*.

Retrograde Planets

The Planets which *appear* to be "backing up" in their orbits, as viewed from the Earth, are marked with R or ℞. Retrograde Planets are no less powerful in their indications than they would be if they were Direct in motion; however, they do seem to indicate more *inner* activity or "going back over" something. *Three or more Natal Planets Retrograde* strongly incline to *introversion*.

Stationary Planets

When a Natal Planet is marked with S for its apparently standing still as seen from the Earth, it is considered to show an outstanding emphasis.

Planets "*At Home*" in the Signs They Rule

Planets placed in the Signs which they rule express in a manner that is *typical*. A Natal Planet at Home in its own Sign is like the actor who is playing a typical role, one in which he feels at home. (Fig. 1 on page 9 shows the Planets in the Signs where they are at home.) Always give emphasis to such Planets.

When a Natal Planet is in the Sign *opposite* a Sign which it rules, it is *not*, I repeat, *not* necessarily any weaker than when in its own Sign. But its role is an *a*typical one, in fact, quite opposite the role it would naturally play.

Planets in Mutual Reception

When there are two Natal Planets in each other's Signs — each Planet placed in a Sign ruled by the other — both Planets are emphasized; they are mutually related in a very harmonious way. Each has somewhat the disposition of the other.

Disposition of Natal Planets

The Ruler of the Sign in which a Natal Planet is placed is said to give its disposition to the Planet(s) placed in its Sign. The Ruler of the Sign is called the Dispositor of any Natal Planet(s) in that Sign.

For more information on Retrograde or Stationary Planets, At Home, Mutual Reception, Disposition, etc. refer to my *Essentials of Natal Interpretation with Study Guide* (A.F.A. Publication).

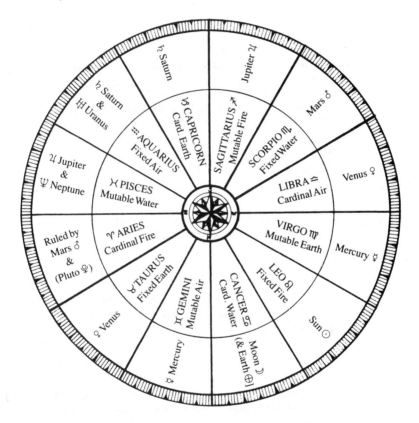

Fig. 1. Signs: Their Elements and Qualities and Planetary Rulers

QUALITIES: Mode of Motion;
Cardinal = Cyclic
Motion; Rim of a wheel;
Fixed = "Non"-Motion; Hub:
Mutable = Sequential Motion; Spoke.

ELEMENTS:
Fire, "emanative," is spontaneous;
Earth, "evidencing," is practical;
Air, "reflective," is animated;
Water, "sustaining," is sensitive.

Odd-numbered Signs (Fire and Air) are masculine, *may* be more extraverted.
Even-numbered Signs (Earth and Water) are feminine, *may* be more introverted.

Some Basic Key-words and Key-phrases for the Signs

Do not make any attempt to memorize these Key-words which are given for reference only; try to get acquainted with the natures of the Signs. *Signs characterize and describe*; consequently, their Key-words and Key-phrases are adjectives or descriptive phrases. There are many other valid Key-words, but the following are nearly always appropriate; these are basic.

Table 1
Some Basic Key-words and Key-phrases for the Signs

♈ ARIES, the 1st Sign: initiating, pioneering, beginning, eager, personal, impetuous, assertive, skeptical, active, etc. Remember Aries is ruled by Mars.*

♉ TAURUS, the 2nd Sign: evaluating, firm, enduring, supportive, acquisitive, possessive, coordinating, steadfast, placid (unless aroused), etc. Venus is Ruler.

♊ GEMINI, the 3rd Sign: dual, varied or variable, simultaneous, communicative in verbal and probably other ways, dexterous, adroit, etc. Mercury is Ruler.

♋ CANCER, the 4th Sign: tenacious, nourishing, sheltering, enveloping, maternal, cherishing, clannish, retrospective, introspective, etc. The Moon is Ruler (and Earth).

♌ LEO, the 5th Sign: hearty, dramatic (or melodramatic!), loyal, direct, dynamic, creative, childlike, romantic, recreational, etc. The Sun is Ruler.

♍ VIRGO, the 6th Sign: analytical, selective, critical, industrious, meticulous, detailed, assimilative, particular, etc. Mercury is the Ruler.

♎ LIBRA, the 7th Sign: complementary, *re*active, cooperative or opposing, companionable, sharing, accommodating, affable, just, etc. Venus is the Ruler.

♏ SCORPIO, the 8th Sign: intense, resourceful, penetrating, productive, generative or regenerative, transitional, desirous, etc. Mars is the Ruler.

♐ SAGITTARIUS, the 9th Sign: seeking, aiming, visualizing, expansive, jovial, religious and/or philosophical, abstract, speculative, etc. Jupiter is the Ruler.

♑ CAPRICORN, the 10th Sign: ambitious, authoritative, controlling, utilizing, serious, formal, effective, etc. Saturn is the Ruler.

♒ AQUARIUS, the 11th Sign: friendly (yet impersonal), advisory, independent, individualistic, informal, original, etc. Saturn and Uranus are co-rulers.

♓ PISCES, the 12th Sign: visionary, mystical, idealistic, elusive, compassionate, imaginative, indefinite, latent. Jupiter and Neptune are the co-rulers.

*I personally accept Pluto as the co-ruler of Aries; some give it to Scorpio.

You have all 12 of the Signs in your complete Natal Chart. Some of the Signs are, however, more emphasized than others in your Chart. Those tenanted by Natal Planets are usually much more emphasized than those which do not contain any Planets. The "Rising Sign" — the Sign which rises on the Eastern Horizon at the time and place of birth — tenanted by Planets or not, is very important to you.

Mutable Signs are often called Dual. Strictly speaking, *Gemini* is dual, doing two things at once; or shifting attention so quickly, the actions seem to be simultaneous. *Virgo* is somewhat like Gemini in this respect. *Pisces* is a Sign of multiplicity rather than duality. *Sagittarius* tends toward more than one interest although not at the same time, for Sagittarius is "single-tracked." All of the Mutable Signs tend to show versatility; they are intermittent in action.

The *Cardinal* Signs are more acute and the *Fixed* more chronic in action or the state described.

The Natural Zodiacal Wheel

Although the Sidereal Zodiac of Constellations is occasionally called the "Natural" Zodiac I am not referring to the Constellations here. Instead, the term "Natural Zodiacal Wheel" means the Wheel in which the Sign Aries, the 1st Sign, occupies its natural place in what is called House 1, at the left of the Wheel. The rest of the Signs follow on around the Wheel (counterclockwise). An entire Sign of 30° occupies each House.

Each House begins with 0° of the Sign allocated to it; consequently, there is no need to mark any degree on any Cusp (beginning point of each House). It is customary to write the glyph for the Sign in its House. If you prefer, you may write 0° of whichever Sign it is at the outside of the Wheel, at the Cusp of the House.

Harriet K. Banes used to call the Natural Zodiacal Wheel "the Wheel of Nature itself, the Wheel of Man, or the Wheel of Humanity." "It shows the natural tendencies," as Carl Leipert stated it.

The HOUSES of the Natural Zodiacal Wheel have certain basic Key-words, such as:

Table 2
Key-words for the Natural Zodiacal Wheel

1st House: Personality, own efforts and own activity, assertiveness, natural approach to life, etc. Mars is the Ruler of this 1st Hosue for everyone; because Aries occupies it. I accept Pluto as co-ruler. Mars may not be *in* the Sign but it *rules* Aries. We do not place the planetary Ruler(s) in the Houses ruled, even though we always bear them in mind.

2nd House: Support, possessiveness, acquisitiveness, endurance, power, etc. Venus is the Ruler.

Table 2 — continued

3rd House: Communicativeness, dexterity, neighborliness, natural sense of kinship, etc. Mercury is the natural Ruler of this House.

4th House: Tenacity, tendency to hold on, clannishness, domesticity, hospitableness, maternal tendencies, etc. The Moon is the Ruler of this House (and Earth).

5th House: Creativity, self-expression, playfulness, centralization, romantic tendencies, etc. The Sun rules this House.

6th House: Selectivity, analysis, assimilation, industriousness, tendency to arrange and adjust, etc. Mercury rules this House.

7th House: Balance, equilibrium, relatedness, tendency to react (especially in cooperation or in competition), etc. Venus rules this House.

8th House: Productivity, resourcefulness, intensity, sexuality, generation, regeneration, transmutation, death or transition, rebirth, etc. Mars rules the 8th.

9th House: Expansiveness, extensiveness, religious tendencies, abstractions, anticipations or tendency to look ahead, etc. Jupiter rules this 9th House.

10th House: ambition, authoritativeness, mastery, tendency to achieve or accomplish, control, etc. Saturn is the Ruler of this 10th House.

11th House: friendliness, hopefulness, independence, tendency toward *knowing* — not just thinking or believing, etc. Saturn and Uranus co-rule this 11th House.

12th House: Mysticism, symbolism, privacy, tendency to conceal or to reveal, latency, the unknown, etc. Jupiter and Neptune co-rule this 12th House.

These Houses of the Natural Zodiacal Wheel (also called the Flat Chart) must not be interpreted the way Radix Houses in the calculated Chart for the exact time and place of birth are interpreted. The Natural Zodiacal Wheel indicates natural tendencies (both conscious and unconscious) and natural characteristics. Whereas the Radix House VII indicates actual partners in the actual world, the 7th House of the Natural Zodiacal Wheel shows the tendency to relate to others. Radix House X indicates the kind of career, major projects, position in life, etc.; but the 10th of the Natural Zodiacal Wheel shows the kind of ambition, the tendency to achieve, etc.

The important point to remember is this: *Natural Zodiacal Wheel Houses* indicate *characteristics, natural tendencies,* etc.; they are *purely subjective,* not objective at all.

SOME DIVISIONS OF THE ZODIAC

The Structuring of the Zodiac of Signs

These Preliminaries provide a foundation for the beginner and a review for the more advanced student of Astrology.

There are four definite points in the Sun's apparent annual cycle which can be determined every year: where the Sun is on the Celestial Equator, at which point it goes into North Declination (the Vernal Equinox); where the Sun is at its point farthest North (the Summer Solstice); where the Sun apparently crosses the Celestial Equator again, crossing this time into South Declination, (at the Fall Equinox); and where the Sun is at the point farthest South (the Winter Solstice).

Fig. 2 shows the Celestial Equator, the Ecliptic (apparent path of the Sun), and the four points mentioned. (If you are disconcerted by the placement of the directions, please turn to face the South; now the East is at your left and the West is at your right. Astrological chart forms are oriented in the same way as this Fig. 2.)

These seasons correspond to the Northern Hemisphere.

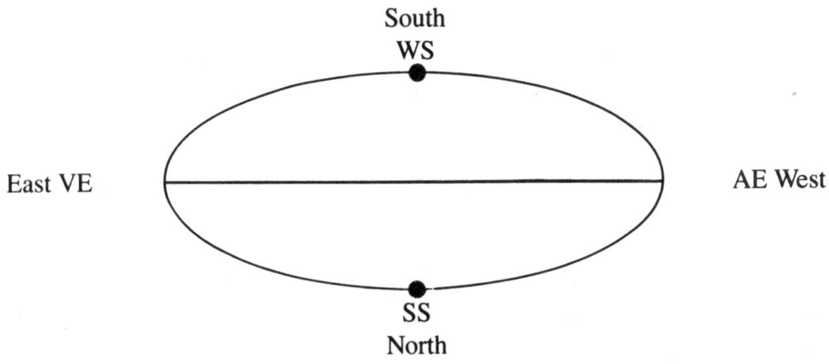

Fig. 2. Structure of the Zodiac

VE AE = the Celestial Equator (half of the circle is shown)
VE, SS, AE, WS, VE = the Ecliptic, the apparent path of the Sun
VE = Vernal (Spring) Equinox, when Sun is on the Celestial Equator
SS = Summer Solstice, when Sun is farthest North in Declination
AE = Autumnal Equinox, when Sun is again on the Celestial Equator
WS = Winter Solstice, when Sun is farthest South in Declination

14

The beginning of this Tropical Zodiac was set at the Vernal Equinox point. 0° of the SIGN Aries was allocated to this point. This is always the beginning of this "Fixed" Zodiac, regardless of where it may be in relation to the Constellations. The Ram leads the rest of the Signs.

0° of the SIGN Cancer was allocated to the Summer Solstice; the Crab's sidling motion was comparable to the Sun's motion at this turning point.

0° of the SIGN Libra was allocated to the Autumnal Equinox; the Scales balance the day and the night at this point as well as dividing the Ecliptic into equal halves. This is 180° from the beginning at 0° Aries.

0° of the SIGN Capricorn was allocated to the Winter Solstice when the Sun is at its height. The mountain Goat climbs to the peaks.

These four Signs mark the four cardinal points on the compass; they are called the Cardinal Signs.

These Signs were considered to be of the nature of the Elements: Aries that of Fire, Libra that of Air; these Signs and Elements complement each other. Cancer is that of Water, Capricorn, that of Earth; these Signs and Elements complement each other.

The Zodiac of Signs

After the circle was quartered at the four "natural" points, each quarter of 90° was trisected. Thus, there are twelve segments of the circle; each one contains exactly 30°. They were called SIGNS of the Zodiac to distinguish them from the 12 Zodiacal Constellations whose names they were given.

The Signs are uniform in size, each containing exactly 30°. The Constellations vary in shape and size, some having more than 30°, others less.

Numbers had great significance to those of the ancient world. This is not the place to enter into the study of Numbers, fascinating though it is.

FOUR was the number of the cardinal directions and of the four Elements. It is true that to those in some parts of the world the Elements are five instead of four; but to those who structured our Zodiac, there were four Elements. FOUR is often associated with foundations; "foursquare" is unyielding and firm. FOUR is often emphasized in the composition of Mandalas. In the Hebrew Alphabet the 4th letter is Daleth which means "door"; it has the numerical value of FOUR.

THREE is a number of great significance also. It is the Trinity. In fact, it is many trinities: thesis, antithesis, synthesis; trefoil, whether a clover or similar plant or even an ornament which symbolizes Trinity; and so on. And in the Hebrew Alphabet the 3rd letter is Gimel which means "camel"; it has the numerical value of THREE. This is especially interesting to me, astrologically speaking: when the Signs are categorized by Four (the four Elements), they are also categorized by "Qualities" which are three in number.

What are the Qualities? They are called the "modes of motion." They are the Cardinal, Fixed, and Mutable Qualities (modes of motion). You already know the Cardinal Signs: Aries, Cancer, Libra, and Capricorn. They are in this order: Cardinal, Fixed, Mutable, continuing around the circle. The Elements too have a certain regular order: Fire, Earth, Air, Water.

Table 3
Elements of Signs

♈ Aries	— Cardinal	Fire	opposite	♎ Libra	— Cardinal	Air
♉ Taurus	— Fixed	Earth	"	♏ Scorpio	— Fixed	Water
♊ Gemini	— Mutable	Air	"	♐ Sagittarius	— Mutable	Fire
♋ Cancer	— Cardinal	Water	"	♑ Capricorn	— Cardinal	Earth
♌ Leo	— Fixed	Fire	"	♒ Aquarius	— Fixed	Air
♍ Virgo	— Mutable	Earth	"	♓ Pisces	— Mutable	Water

Fire and Air are opposite and complementary; so with Earth and Water. Only one Sign (Aries) is both Cardinal and Fire; only one is Fixed Earth, . . . We shall have more about the *meanings* of these categories as we proceed.

The Sun, Moon, Planets, and other points which we wish to indicate are located by their Celestial Longitude in the Signs, noted by ° (degrees) ' (minutes) and, sometimes, " (seconds) of space.

Alan Leo, in his *Dictionary of Astrology* (American Federation of Astrologers, Tempe, Ariz. 85282) described this Zodiac of Signs as "an imaginary circle passing round the earth in the plane of the ecliptic." Elsewhere (sorry, I can't recall the exact source of this) Alan Leo said something to the effect that the Zodiac of Signs is within the aura of Earth, that is, the magnetic field of Earth. So the Sun, Moon, and Planets relate to us on Earth according to their Sign positions. Incidentally, when planting by the Moon, it is absolutely necessary to use the Moon's position in the SIGN instead of in the Constellation of the same name.

36 Decanates of the Zodiac

One of the most widely used divisions of the zodiacal Sign is the Decanate. There are 36 Decanates of the Zodiac; that is, 3 Decanates within each Sign. Each Decanate (frequently called Decan) consists of 10° of space.

The 1st Decan of any Sign begins at 00° 00' 00" of that Sign.
The 2nd Decan of any Sign begins at 10° 00' 00" of that Sign.
The 3rd Decan of any Sign begins at 20° 00' 00" of that Sign.
Because Carl Leipert considered that both types of Rulers of the Decans are valid, I am listing both:

16

Table 4 — Rulers of Decans

Sign		Decan			Ruler (per Leo)		"Ruler" (per Sepharial)	
♈	Aries	1st:	Aries	♈	♂	Mars	♂	Mars
	Aries	2nd:	Leo	♌	☉	Sun	☉	Sun
	Aries	3rd:	Sagittarius	♐	♃	Jupiter	♀	Venus
♉	Taurus	1st:	Taurus	♉	♀	Venus	☿	Mercury
	Taurus	2nd:	Virgo	♍	☿	Mercury	☽	Moon
	Taurus	3rd:	Capricorn	♑	♄	Saturn	♄	Saturn
♊	Gemini	1st:	Gemini	♊	☿	Mercury	♃	Jupiter
	Gemini	2nd:	Libra	♎	♀	Venus	♂	Mars
	Gemini	3rd:	Aquarius	♒	♄	Saturn*	☉	Sun
♋	Cancer	1st:	Cancer	♋	☽	Moon	♀	Venus
	Cancer	2nd:	Scorpio	♏	♂	Mars	☿	Mercury
	Cancer	3rd:	Pisces	♓	♃	Jupiter**	☽	Moon
♌	Leo	1st:	Leo	♌	☉	Sun	♄	Saturn
	Leo	2nd:	Sagittarius	♐	♃	Jupiter	♃	Jupiter
	Leo	3rd:	Aries	♈	♂	Mars	♂	Mars
♍	Virgo	1st:	Virgo	♍	☿	Mercury	☉	Sun
	Virgo	2nd:	Capricorn	♑	♄	Saturn	♀	Venus
	Virgo	3rd:	Taurus	♉	♀	Venus	☿	Mercury
♎	Libra	1st:	Libra	♎	♀	Venus	☽	Moon
	Libra	2nd:	Aquarius	♒	♄	Saturn*	♄	Saturn
	Libra	3rd:	Gemini	♊	☿	Mercury	♃	Jupiter
♏	Scorpio	1st:	Scorpio	♏	♂	Mars	♂	Mars
	Scorpio	2nd:	Pisces	♓	♃	Jupiter**	☉	Sun
	Scorpio	3rd:	Cancer	♋	☽	Moon	♀	Venus
♐	Sagittartius	1st:	Sagittarius	♐	♃	Jupiter	☿	Mercury
	Sagittarius	2nd:	Aries	♈	♂	Mars	☽	Moon
	Sagittarius	3rd:	Leo	♌	☉	Sun	♄	Saturn
♑	Capricorn	1st:	Capricorn	♑	♄	Saturn	♃	Jupiter
	Capricorn	2nd:	Taurus	♉	♀	Venus	♂	Mars
	Capricorn	3rd:	Virgo	♍	☿	Mercury	☉	Sun
♒	Aquarius	1st:	Aquarius	♒	♄	Saturn*	♀	Venus
	Aquarius	2nd:	Gemini	♊	☿	Mercury	☿	Mercury
	Aquarius	3rd:	Libra	♎	♀	Venus	☽	Moon
♓	Pisces	1st:	Pisces	♓	♃	Jupiter**	♄	Saturn
	Pisces	2nd:	Cancer	♋	☽	Moon	♃	Jupiter
	Pisces	3rd:	Scorpio	♏	♂	Mars	♂	Mars

* Saturn was formerly called the Ruler of Aquarius. In modern times, Uranus, considered to be co-ruler, may be added.

**Jupiter was formerly called the Ruler of Pisces. Now, Neptune, the co-ruler, may be added.

Uranus, Neptune, and Pluto are not to be included in Sepharial's Chaldean arrangement.

The Decanates (Decans)

Alan Leo preferred the allocations of the Decans in the Signs according to the Triplicities (Elements). Aries is a Fire Sign; so its Decans are named after the Fire Signs: 1st Decan, Aries; 2nd, Leo; 3rd, Sagittarius. In Taurus (an Earth Sign) the 1st Dean is Taurus; the 2nd, Virgo; the 3rd, Capricorn. Always — in any Sign — begin with the name of the Sign itself; continue in the order of the Signs, including each of the Signs of the same Element. The planetary Ruler of the corresponding Sign is considered a Ruler of the Decanate.*

Sepharial, an equally noted British Astrologer, preferred another set of Rulers of the Decans. He used the Planets in their so-called Chaldean Order (Saturn, Jupiter, Mars, Sun, Venus, Mercury, and the Moon), beginning with Mars for the 1st Decan of Aries.** See Table 34 in Appendix I for a substitute for Table 4.

As you look over the lists again you see that some Decans are given the same Planets by both Leo and Sepharial. However, for most of the Decans the two listings of Planets are not the same. Let me tell you what Leipert did then:

Suppose you have a Natal Planet in the 3rd Decan of the *Sign Aries*. Signs describe; so that Planet expresses in an eager, pioneering, assertive way (some of the Key-words for Aries). *The disposition of the entire Sign is martial* (Mars is the Ruler of the entire Sign). The *3rd Decan of Aries* is of a somewhat Sagittarian nature (although *it is still Aries,* which must not be forgotten!) with an expansive, goal-oriented, more philosophical accent. We do not go so far as to say that Jupiter — Ruler of the Sign Sagittarius, with which the 3rd Decan of the Sign Aries is associated — is a Dispositor of any Planets located in this Decan, there does seem to be *a slightly jupiterian tinge* to the martial Disposition. Do you see how you can blend — with more emphasis on the Ruler of the Sign itself and just a "tinge" on the Ruler of the Sign

---

* Re Ruler (per Leo): These Rulers of the Decanates are the Rulers of the Signs to which the Decanates correspond. Of course, the Ruler of the Sign itself is given precedence over the Ruler of the Decanate. In fact, the Decanate must be remembered to be a portion of the Sign; it is *not* of greater importance than the Sign itself. The Ruler of the Decan (as given by *Leo*) might well be considered to be a kind of sub-ruler of the Sign throughout its 10° portion.

**Re Ruler (per Sepharial): Leipert would not accept the Planets listed here as Rulers of the Decans. For Rulers, he used those as given by Alan Leo. Nevertheless, Leipert was convinced that those given by Sepharial — while not Rulers — were unquestionably "connected in some way" with the Decans.

associated with the Decan — the Mars with an "accent" of Jupiter? An actual example, later, will clarify this point.

Now, in case we wish to note which Planet Sepharial associated with this same Decan of Aries, we look in Table 4 (page 16) under Sepharial: *Venus* is listed. Leipert did not call this a Ruler of the Decan; but he did state we can see a "connection" or an "association" of some kind between this Decan and the Planet Venus. He found that such a Planet could give valuable clues in the interpretation of Charts, markedly in Horary Astrology.

Many people interpret Planets in Signs proficiently without any consideration whatever of the Decanates. The Decan is not an essential of natal interpretation. However, the inclusion of the Decan does help greatly to understand more of what Leipert called "the background."

Leipert suggested that we make a special study of the Decan occupied by the Natal Sun. With what Sign does yours correspond? (If not already familiar with the Natures of the Signs, please review the Key-words and phrases given in Table 1.)

Describe your Natal Sun by its Sign position. . . . Now, *supplement* by some appropriate Key-words and phrases for the Sign which corresponds to the Decan occupied by your Natal Sun. You may continue on with all the other Natal Planets; but most important is this treatment of the Natal Sun.

The FACES

The term "FACE" may properly be applied to two different subdivisions of Signs. Perhaps I should have said "FACES" instead of "FACE" because they mark distinctions between Positive and Negative. Some symonyms for Positive, as used here: masculine, active, acting upon, electric, etc. Some synonyms for Negative, as the complement to Positive, are: feminine, passive, acted upon, magnetic, etc. You understand that "Negative" is not used in any derogatory sense here; it might well be called the *Yin*; while the Positive Faces correspond to the *Yang*. And, in this way, the Positive is the Creative; the Negative, the Receptive.

The Signs themselves were considered by the ancients to be Positive and Negative, Masculine and Feminine. The odd-numbered Signs are Positive (Masculine): Aries, Gemini, Leo, Libra, Sagittarius, Aquarius. The even-numbered Signs, Taurus, Cancer, Virgo, Scorpio, Capricorn, Pisces, the Negative (Feminine).

By the way, *Libra,* an odd-numbered sign — Masculine, but, ruled by the feminine Venus, is the least masculine of the Masculine Signs. Neither the Sun nor Mars plays a typical role in Libra with its venusian Disposition. Either the Sun or Mars in Libra may play a powerful role, but not a typical one; for any Planet in Libra has the Disposition of Venus, its Ruler.

Also, *Scorpio,* an even-numbered Sign — Feminine, but, ruled by the masculine Mars, is the least feminine of all the Feminine Signs. Neither the Moon nor Venus plays a typical role here; because any Planet in Scorpio has the Disposition of Mars, its Ruler. We might state this somewhat differently.

Libra, though a Masculine Sign, expresses more of the Feminine Disposition than do the other Masculine Signs. *Scorpio,* although Feminine, expresses more of the Masculine Disposition than do the other Feminine even-numbered Signs.

The FACES; FACES of the Signs

Each zodiacal Sign (30°) is divided into two Faces of 15° each. Thus, we have 24 of these Faces. The first half of *each odd-number Sign* is Masculine or *Yang* or Positive. The second half is Feminine or *Yin* or Negative.

The first half of *each even-numbered Sign* is Feminine or *Yin* or Negative. The second half is Masculine or *Yang* or Positive.

I don't think it necessary to list all twelve Signs here because this pattern applies throughout the Zodiac. Be sure the Sign in which you are interested is in the odd-numbered or even-numbered category.

Table 5
Faces of the Signs

In the *odd*-numbered Signs:
00° 00' 00" begins the 1st Face of the Sign. It is + . (+ represents Positive.)
15° 00' 00" begins the 2nd Face of the Sign. It is − . (− represents Negative.)
In the *even*-numbered Signs:
00° 00' 00" begins the 1st Face of the Sign. It is − .
15° 00' 00" begins the 2nd Face of the Sign. It is + .

These Divisions are exact; they do not allow for any Orb. 14° 59' 59" is still in the 1st Face of the Sign. Then 15° 00' 00" begins the 2nd Face of the Sign.

To summarize: the first half of an odd-numbered Sign is the + half and the second half is the − half. The first half of an even-numbered Sign is the − half and the second half is the + half.

The Face of a Sign consists of exactly 15° of space.

There is another Division which is called FACE; this, however, is the Face of a *Decanate.* Each Decan (Decanate) consists of 10°. Each Decanate has two Faces: one that is + (Positive) and one that is − (Negative).

The Face of a Decan consists of exactly 5 degrees.

Table 6
Faces of the Decans

In the *odd*-numbered Signs:
00° 00' 00" begins the 1st Face of the 1st Decan. It is + .
05° 00' 00" begins the 2nd Face of the 1st Decan. It is − .
10° 00' 00" begins the 1st Face of the 2nd Decan. It is − .
15° 00' 00" begins the 2nd Face of the 2nd Decan. It is + .
20° 00' 00" begins the 1st Face of the 3rd Decan. It is + .
25° 00' 00" begins the 2nd Face of the 3rd Decan. It is − .
In the *even*-numbered Signs:
00° 00' 00" begins the 1st Face of the 1st Decan. It is − .
05° 00' 00" begins the 2nd Face of the 1st Decan. It is + .
10° 00' 00" begins the 1st Face of the 2nd Decan. It is + .
15° 00' 00" begins the 2nd Face of the 2nd Decan. It is − .
20° 00' 00" begins the 1st Face of the 3rd Decan. It is − .
25° 00' 00" begins the 2nd Face of the 3rd Decan. It is + .

Now let us summarize all these + s and − s.

Table 7
Summary of Tables 5 and 6

An *odd*-numbered Sign: Faces of the Signs
00° 00' 00" begins the + Sign (consists of 30°):
00° 00' 00" begins the + Face (consists of 15°) of the Sign:
00° 00' 00" begins the + Face of the 1st Decan,
05° 00' 00" begins the − Face of the 1st Decan,
10° 00' 00" begins the − Face of the 2nd Decan,
15° 00' 00" begins the − Face (consists of 15°) of the Sign:
15° 00' 00" begins the + Face of the 2nd Decan,
20° 00' 00" begins the + Face of the 3rd Decan,
25° 00' 00" begins the − Face of the 3rd Decan.
An *even*-numbered Sign:
00° 00' 00" begins the the − Sign (consists of 30°):
00° 00' 00" begins the − Face (consists of 15°) of the Sign:
00° 00' 00" begins the − Face of the 1st Decan,
05° 00' 00" begins the + Face of the 1st Decan,
10° 00' 00" begins the + Face of the 2nd Decan,
15° 00' 00" begins the + Face (consists of 15°) of the Sign:
15° 00' 00" begins the − Face of the 2nd Decan,
20° 00' 00" begins the − Face of the 3rd Decan,
25° 00' 00" begins the + Face of the 3rd Decan.

The above given Subdivisions as to + (Positive) and − (Negative) are shown on Fig. 3. After you become familiar with the "pattern" of + and −, as shown above, you won't need to refer to the Fig. 3; just be sure the Sign is odd-numbered or even-numbered.

Are you wondering if it is worthwhile to bother with all these + s and − s?

Frankly, this is not an essential of natal interpretation. Nevertheless, this classification of Natal Planets (and the Radix Ascendant when known) may be quite significant.

As an example we'll use the Natal Planets along with the Radix Ascendant of Bernard Baruch whose Charts were used in my *Side Lights of Astrology, Essentials of Natal Interpretation with Study Guide,* and *The Star Wheel.*

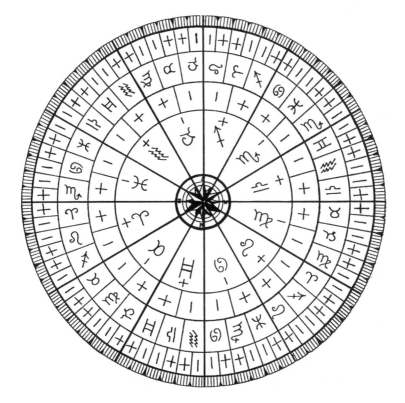

Fig. 3. Diagram — Positive and Negative Areas

The innermost Wheel is that of the odd-numbered and even-numbered Positive and Negative Signs (30° each). Next are the Positive and Negative Faces of these Signs (15° each). Next are the Decans (10° each); then, the Positive and Negative Faces of the Decans (05° each). Outside are the 360° of the Zodiac.

Example: Natal Planets (and Radix Asc.) of Bernard Baruch: (see Fig. 17, page 53).

Table 8 Natal Planets in the Faces

Natal Position	Sign	Face of Sign	Decan	Face of Decan
☉ 26° ♌ 32′ 22″	+	−	♈	−
⊕ 26° ♒ 32′ 22″	+	−	♎	−
☽ 01° ♊ 44′	+	+	♊	+
☿ 17° ♍ 08′	−	+	♑	−
♀ 28° ♋ 43′	−	+	♓	+
♂ 17° ♋ 16′	−	+	♏	−
♃ 21° ♊ 43′	+	−	♒	+
♄ 21° ♐ 58′ ℞	+	−	♌	+
♅ 24° ♋ 24′	−	+	♓	−
♆ 21° ♈ 42′ ℞	+	−	♐	+
♇ 18° ♉ 47′ ℞	−	+	♍	−
A. 11° ♐ 05′	+	+	♈	−

Now that we have the above information, how can se use it?

Geraldine Davis, author of *Horary Astrology,* said she always used the Faces of the Decans in Natal Astrology and frequently in Horary Astrology.

Carl Leipert did not consider this an *essential*; but, whenever he made such a classification, he always used all three (Sign, Face of the Sign, and Face of the Decan). He gave the greatest emphasis to the Sign itself, as Positive; or as Negative.

Unless we have some way to evaluate the + s and − s, the above listing doesn't indicate enough. My suggestion is that we allocate certain "values" to each classification:

In other words, we give a value of 1 to the Face of a Decan, a value of 6 to a Sign, and a value of 3 to the Face of a Sign. It is a rather arbitrary evaluation, but one I have found to be both reasonable and effective. Let us apply it:

Mr. Baruch's Natal Planets (⊕, Earth, included) occupy 6 + Signs and 5 − Signs; 6 + Faces of Signs and 5 −; 5 + Faces of Decans and 6 − . You see this is difficult to evaluate. However, by multiplying the + s and − s in Signs by 6, those in Faces of Signs by 3, and those in Faces of Decans by 1, we have a clearer evaluation.

+s	−s
6 times 6 = 36 + s in Signs	5 times 6 = 30 − s in Signs
6 times 3 = 18 + s in Sign-Faces	5 times 3 = 15 − s in Sign-Faces
5 times 1 = _5_ + s in Decan-Faces	6 times 1 = _6_ − s in Decan-Faces
59 value of + s (Planets)	51 value of − s (Planets)
_9_ value of + s (Asc.)	_1_ value of − (Asc.)
68 value of + s	52 value of − s

This evaluation shows a quite definite, but not excessive, emphasis on the + s. So Mr. Baruch would incline to be more creative than receptive, more active than passive, more act*ing* upon than act*ed* upon; perhaps more inclined to extraversion than to introversion (although for this, also check Retrograde Planets; three or more Retrograde Natal Planets tend toward introversion).

THE 144 DUODENARY DIVISIONS

These Duodenary Divisions of the Zodiac may be more familiar under the name given them by the Hindu astrologers — Dwadashamsa or Dwadasamsa, usually abbreviated "Dwad" in the western world of Astrology.

Leipert used the term Duodenary although he said "Duodecimal" would be equally accurate; each term means "twelfth."

Manilius, the Roman astrologer, used the term Dodecatemorion for this 2½° division, the twelfth part of a Sign. (The National Astrological Library, Washington, D.C., republished [in 1953] *The Five Books of M. Manilius*.) This is a translation by Thomas Creech into English verse, first published back in 1696. The Latin original was the work of Manilius, a contemporary of Augustus Caesar. If not fond of reading verse, you'd likely be interested in the contents of this remarkable book. If you enjoy verse, you'll probably be delighted. It contains a great deal of worthwhile material. Although there is so much material given by Manilius that is of value today, the sections on the Dodecatemoria are the especially pertinent ones to us here.

While still in Europe Leipert became acquainted with the work of Manilius; I believe that it was the basis for his great interest in the Dwads. He was familiar enough with Hindu Astrology to have a high regard for its antiquity and its ancient wisdom. He experimented with their various Divisions of the Signs and so on. He recognized that each Zodiac — the Sidereal Zodiac of Constellations and the Tropical Zodiac of Signs — has its own validity.

Leipert gave due credit to the Hindus for the Dwads; but he also contended that the Dwads must have been known and used by the Chaldean astrologers as well. The Astrology which had its probable origin in the Tigro-Euphrates Valley has come to us by way of the Greek, Roman, Arabian, medieval and later European astrologers — plus others in the various parts of the so-called "western" world. I do not say that our "western" Astrology (meaning Tropical Zodiac Astrology) is the only true Astrology; but this is the kind we are studying here. Remember, there are many valid kinds of Astrology — Hindu, Chinese, Tibetan, . . . and how many others? as well as that with which we are familiar.

The 144 Duodenary Divisions of the Zodiac

Each Sign contains 30°. The 12th Part of a Sign consists of 02° 30′.

There are 12 Signs in the Zodiac. There are, in all, 144 Duodenary Divisions.

Leipert frequently referred to these Dwads as "Doors" of Consciousness as well as very important "focal areas."

Leipert continued to use the Decans also; but he made this important distinction: the Decan shows a kind of coloring or modification; it gives a kind of background to the Dwad. The Dwad gives "the specifics and particulars." Of course, the meanings of the Sign itself must not be overlooked!

The concept of the Dwads is not a modern one; in western Astrology it goes back to Manilius, undoubtedly to a period before his time, because *The Five Books* were a summary in verse of astrological material that was old in his day.

But Leipert made a practical use of the Dwads, acquiring a special fluency in his interpretation of Planets and House Cusps when he delineated any kind of calculated Chart — Natal, Mundane or Horary. He noted the Transits of the Planets in the Dwads occupied day by day: especially, the Dwad occupied by Eclipses, New and Full Moons, and Planetary Stations — Retrograde and Direct — in order to include "the specifics and particulars."

"THERE IS A ZODIAC WITHIN EACH SIGN."

"THERE IS ALSO A WHEEL OF HOUSES WITHIN EACH SIGN."

This Table is reproduced from the one given on page 29 of my *Side Lights of Astrology*.

Table 9
Duodenary Divisions of Signs

The Dwadasamsas (Dvadasamsas) — The "Zodiac" Within Each and Every Sign:

Division	Signs "Dwads."	♈	♉	♊	♋	♌	♍	♎	♏	♐	♑	♒	♓
1st	0°	♈	♉	♊	♋	♌	♍	♎	♏	♐	♑	♒	♓
2nd	2½°	♉	♊	♋	♌	♍	♎	♏	♐	♑	♒	♓	♈
3rd	5°	♊	♋	♌	♍	♎	♏	♐	♑	♒	♓	♈	♉
4th	7½°	♋	♌	♍	♎	♏	♐	♑	♒	♓	♈	♉	♊
5th	10°	♌	♍	♎	♏	♐	♑	♒	♓	♈	♉	♊	♋
6th	12½°	♍	♎	♏	♐	♑	♒	♓	♈	♉	♊	♋	♌
7th	15°	♎	♏	♐	♑	♒	♓	♈	♉	♊	♋	♌	♍
8th	17½°	♏	♐	♑	♒	♓	♈	♉	♊	♋	♌	♍	♎
9th	20°	♐	♑	♒	♓	♈	♉	♊	♋	♌	♍	♎	♏
10th	22½°	♑	♒	♓	♈	♉	♊	♋	♌	♍	♎	♏	♐
11th	25°	♒	♓	♈	♉	♊	♋	♌	♍	♎	♏	♐	♑
12th	27½°	♓	♈	♉	♊	♋	♌	♍	♎	♏	♐	♑	♒

The glyphs for the Signs are given in a horizontal line across the top.
The glyphs for the Dwads are listed under each Sign.
The 1st Duodenary Division of a Sign begins at 00° 00′ 00″ .
The 2nd Duodenary Division of a Sign begins at 02° 30′ 00″ .
The 3rd Duodenary Division of a Sign begins at 05° 00′ 00″ .

Suppose an example Natal Sun is at 02° 29′ 59″ of Capricorn. Look for the glyph for Capricorn, ♑, in the line of Signs at the top of the Table. Look for the correct Duodenary Division (in this example, the one which begins at 0°) and find the intersection with the column headed by the Sign Capricorn; this gives ♑ as the required Dwad, the Capricorn Dwad in the Sign Capricorn. Had the example Sun been 02° 30′ 00″ of Capricorn, the required Dwad would have been the 2nd, ♒, that of Aquarius, in the Sign Capricorn.

Let us return to our example: Bernard Baruch's Natal Sun is 26° Leo 32′ 22″. 26° 32′ 22″ is in the Dwad which begins at 25°, the 11th Duodenary Division. His Sun is in the Sign Leo. So, follow across from the 11th Division till you intersect the column for the Sign Leo; there is shown the Gemini Dwad.

Now, suppose you wish to know how many Natal Planets are in the 9th Duodenary Divisions of Signs? What is the area in each and every Sign? The 9th Division begins at 20° in any Sign. We refer to the list of his Natal Planets (on page 22). His Neptune, Jupiter, and Saturn all occupy some 9th Division: Neptune in the Sagittarian Dwad of Aries, Jupiter in the Aquarian Dwad of Gemini, and Saturn in the Leonian Dwad of Sagittarius. (It is more usual to say "the Aquarius Dwad" than "the Aquarian Dwad." However, the choice is yours!)

Given above are three different ways of looking up Dwads in this Table.

Fig. 4 is reproduced from my *The Star Wheel: "Wheels within Wheels"* in which it was Plate "J".

"A Zodiac within Each Sign"

We know there are exactly 30° of celestial Longitude in each Sign of the Zodiac. When any sign is divided into 12 Parts — Dwads, each Dwad partakes of the nature of a Sign and House with which it is related in the Zodiac of Signs and the Wheel of Houses. In other words, each 2½° portion of a Sign corresponds to some Sign in the Zodiac and to some House in the Wheel.

In such an arrangement, each 2½° arc represents an entire Sign and a House.

A Natal Planet is analyzed more fully by its being located in the Dwad occupied as well as in the Sign occupied. Each Dwad is a significant "focal area" within the Sign itself. Each Dwad "pinpoints" precisely and focuses upon some detail, feature, or highlight which might have been overlooked in the overall interpretation of the Sign itself. Of course, the basic meanings of the Sign itself must not be subordinated to the meanings of the Dwads! Instead, the meanings of the Signs are enhanced by the inclusion of the meanings of the Dwads.

The "Dwad-Signs"

"There is a Zodiac within each Sign."

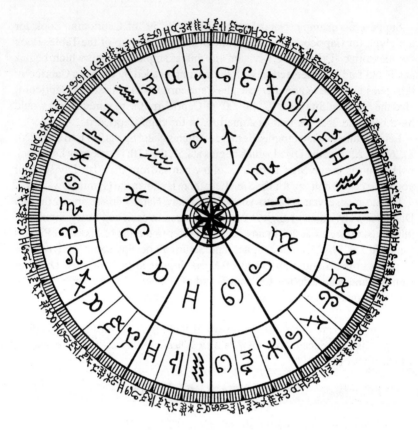

Fig. 4. Diagram — Signs, Decans, and Dwads

The zodiacal Circle contains 360°; it consists of 12 Signs of 30° each.
Each Sign contains 3 Decans of 10° each.
Each Decan contains 4 Dwads of 2° 30′ each.
Each Sign contains 12 Dwads. There are 144 Dwads in the Zodiac.

"There are 12 Dwad-Signs within each Sign." That is to say: each 2½° arc
of a Sign is called a "Dwad-Sign" when the focus is interpreted as if it were
the corresponding Sign. Each Dwad-Sign has characteristics very much like
those of that Sign with which it corresponds (of the same name).

For example: Mr. Baruch's Natal Sun is in the Gemini Dwad-Sign of Leo.
His Sun is described by the Key-words of Leo for the overall picture. The
interpretation, however, is enhanced by Key-words for the Dwad-Sign Gemini;
because there is this focus upon the part of Leo which has correspondences
with the Sign Gemini.

The "Dwad-Houses"

"There is a Wheel of Houses within each Sign."

"There are 12 Dwad-Houses within each Sign." That is to say: each 2½° arc of a Sign is called a "Dwad-House" when the focus is interpreted as if it were the corresponding House. Each Dwad-House is given meanings very much like those of that House with which it corresponds (House number). For example: Mr. Baruch's Natal Sun is in the 11th Dwad-House of Leo. Regardless of the actual House occupied in his Radix Chart — wherever it may be — it is very much as if his Sun occupied House XI. We'll go into this more fully as we proceed.

It is advisable to interpret all the Natal Planets in the Dwad-Signs and the Dwad-Houses they occupy. It is especially important to analyze the Natal Sun in this way. This does not complicate your interpretation; instead, it clarifies much. Moreover, the Dwad-Signs and Dwad-Houses offer greater relatedness of the many factors to be considered; they show connections between and among Natal Planets that might appear to be totally unrelated otherwise.

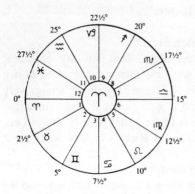

THE SIGN ARIES

Element: Fire
Quality: Cardinal
Disposition: martial
Ruler: Mars
  (I give Pluto as Co-ruler)

Aries contains 30°
It is divided into 12 Dwads
Each Dwad contains 2½°

Fig. 5. The Wheel and Zodiac in Aries

Table 10
Sign Aries

Dwad-House*	Dwad-Sign**	Quality & Element of Dwad-Sign		"Sub-ruler"
1st	Aries	Cardinal	Fire	Mars (& Pluto)
2nd	Taurus	Fixed	Earth	Venus
3rd	Gemini	Mutable	Air	Mercury
4th	Cancer	Cardinal	Water	Moon (& Earth)
5th	Leo	Fixed	Fire	Sun
6th	Virgo	Mutable	Earth	Mercury
7th	Libra	Cardinal	Air	Venus
8th	Scorpio	Fixed	Water	Mars
9th	Sagittarius	Mutable	Fire	Jupiter
10th	Capricorn	Cardinal	Earth	Saturn
11th	Aquarius	Fixed	Air	Saturn & Uranus
12th	Pisces	Mutable	Water	Jupiter & Neptune

 * Each Dwad-House corresponds to the House which has the same Number.
**Each Dwad-Sign corresponds to the Sign which has the same Name.
Some Accentuations and Modifications:
The 1st, 5th, and 9th Dwads in Aries accentuate the Fire Element.
The 1st, 4th, 7th, and 10th Dwads in Aries accentuate the Cardinal Quality.
The 1st and 8th Dwads in Aries accentuate the martial Disposition.
The 2nd, 5th, 8th, and 11th Dwads in Aries have a "tinge of Fixity."
The 2nd and 7th Dwads in Aries are somewhat venusian, not so martial.
  The Dwads do not change the nature of the Sign; they accentuate and modify the interpretation. All of Aries is arian.

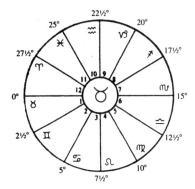

THE SIGN TAURUS

Element: Earth
Quality: Fixed
Disposition: venusian
Ruler: Venus

Taurus contains 30°
It is divided into 12 Dwads
Each Dwad contains 2½°

Fig. 6. The Wheel and Zodiac in Taurus

Table 11
Sign Taurus

Dwad-House*	Dwad-Sign**	Quality & Element of Dwad-Sign		"Sub-ruler"
1st	Taurus	Fixed	Earth	Venus
2nd	Gemini	Mutable	Air	Mercury
3rd	Cancer	Cardinal	Water	Moon (& Earth)
4th	Leo	Fixed	Fire	Sun
5th	Virgo	Mutable	Earth	Mercury
6th	Libra	Cardinal	Air	Venus
7th	Scorpio	Fixed	Water	Mars
8th	Sagittarius	Mutable	Fire	Jupiter
9th	Capricorn	Cardinal	Earth	Saturn
10th	Aquarius	Fixed	Air	Saturn & Uranus
11th	Pisces	Mutable	Water	Jupiter & Neptune
12th	Aries	Cardinal	Fire	Mars (& Pluto)

* Each Dwad-House corresponds to the House which has the same Number.

**Each Dwad-Sign corresponds to the Sign which has the same Name.

Some Accentuations and Modifications:

The 1st, 5th, and 9th Dwads in Taurus accentuate the Earth Element.

The 1st, 4th, 7th, and 10th Dwads in Taurus accentuate the Fixed Quality.

The 1st and 6th Dwads in Taurus accentuate the venusian Disposition.

The 3rd, 6th, 9th, and 12th Dwads in Taurus (correspond to Cardinal Signs) and the 2nd, 5th, 8th, and 11th Dwads in Taurus (correspond to Mutable Signs) show perhaps less emphasis on Fixity.

The 7th and 12th Dwads in Taurus are somewhat martial, not quite so venusian.

The Dwads do not change the nature of the Sign; they accentuate and modify the interpretation. All of Taurus is taurean.

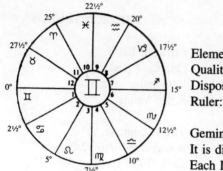

THE SIGN GEMINI

Element: Air
Quality: Mutable
Disposition: mercurial
Ruler: Mercury

Gemini contains 30°
It is divided into 12 Dwads
Each Dwad contains 2½°

Fig. 7. The Wheel and Zodiac in Gemini

Table 12
Sign Gemini

Dwad-House*	Dwad-Sign**	Quality & Element of Dwad-Sign		"Sub-ruler"
1st	Gemini	Mutable	Air	Mercury
2nd	Cancer	Cardinal	Water	Moon (& Earth)
3rd	Leo	Fixed	Fire	Sun
4th	Virgo	Mutable	Earth	Mercury
5th	Libra	Cardinal	Air	Venus
6th	Scorpio	Fixed	Water	Mars
7th	Sagittarius	Mutable	Fire	Jupiter
8th	Capricorn	Cardinal	Earth	Saturn
9th	Aquarius	Fixed	Air	Saturn & Uranus
10th	Pisces	Mutable	Water	Jupiter & Neptune
11th	Aries	Cardinal	Fire	Mars (& Pluto)
12th	Taurus	Fixed	Earth	Venus

* Each Dwad-House corresponds to the House which has the same Number.
**Each Dwad-Sign corresponds to the Sign which has the same Name.
Some Accentuations and Modifications:
The 1st, 5th, and 9th Dwads in Gemini accentuate the Air Element.
The 1st, 4th, 7th, and 10th Dwads in Gemini accentuate the Mutable Quality.
The 1st and 4th Dwads in Gemini accentuate the mercurial Disposition.
The 3rd, 6th, 9th, and 12th Dwads in Gemini have a "tinge of Fixity" (compared to the rest of the Sign Gemini).
The 7th and 10th Dwads in Gemini are somewhat jovial, not quite so mercurial.
The Dwads do not change the nature of the Sign; they accentuate and modify the interpretation. All of Gemini is geminian.

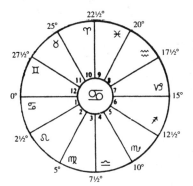

THE SIGN CANCER

Element: Water
Quality: Cardinal
Disposition: lunar
Ruler: Moon (and Earth?)

Cancer contains 30°
It is divided into 12 Dwads
Each Dwad contains 2½°

Fig. 8. The Wheel and Zodiac in Cancer

Table 13
Sign Cancer

Dwad-House*	Dwad-Sign**	Quality & Element of Dwad-Sign		"Sub-ruler"
1st	Cancer	Cardinal	Water	Moon (& Earth)
2nd	Leo	Fixed	Fire	Sun
3rd	Virgo	Mutable	Earth	Mercury
4th	Libra	Cardinal	Air	Venus
5th	Scorpio	Fixed	Water	Mars
6th	Sagittarius	Mutable	Fire	Jupiter
7th	Capricorn	Cardinal	Earth	Saturn
8th	Aquarius	Fixed	Air	Saturn & Uranus
9th	Pisces	Mutable	Water	Jupiter & Neptune
10th	Aries	Cardinal	Fire	Mars (& Pluto)
11th	Taurus	Fixed	Earth	Venus
12th	Gemini	Mutable	Air	Mercury

* Each Dwad-House corresponds to the House which has the same Number.
**Each Dwad-Sign corresponds to the Sign which has the same Name.
Some Accentuations and Modifications:
The 1st, 5th, and 9th Dwads in Cancer accentuate the Water Element.
The 1st, 4th, 7th, and 10th Dwads in Cancer accentuate the Cardinal Quality.
The 1st Dwad in Cancer accentuates the lunar Disposition.
The 2nd, 5th, 8th, and 11th Dwads in Cancer have a "tinge of Fixity" (together with the natural tenacity of the Sign itself).
The 7th and 8th Dwads in Cancer are somewhat saturnian.
The Dwads do not change the nature of the Sign; they accentuate and modify the interpretation. All of Cancer is cancerian.

34

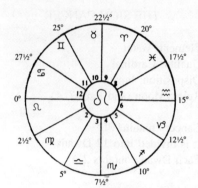

THE SIGN LEO

Element: Fire
Quality: Fixed
Disposition: solar
Ruler: Sun

Leo contains 30°
It is divided into 12 Dwads
Each Dwad contains 2½°

Fig. 9. The Wheel and Zodiac in Leo

Table 14
Sign Leo

Dwad-House*	Dwad-Sign**	Quality & Element of Dwad-Sign		"Sub-ruler"
1st	Leo	Fixed	Fire	Sun
2nd	Virgo	Mutable	Earth	Mercury
3rd	Libra	Cardinal	Air	Venus
4th	Scorpio	Fixed	Water	Mars
5th	Sagittarius	Mutable	Fire	Jupiter
6th	Capricorn	Cardinal	Earth	Saturn
7th	Aquarius	Fixed	Air	Saturn & Uranus
8th	Pisces	Mutable	Water	Jupiter & Neptune
9th	Aries	Cardinal	Fire	Mars (& Pluto)
10th	Taurus	Fixed	Earth	Venus
11th	Gemini	Mutable	Air	Mercury
12th	Cancer	Cardinal	Water	Moon (& Earth)

* Each Dwad-House corresponds to the House which has the same Number.
**Each Dwad-Sign corresponds to the Sign which has the same Name.
Some Accentuations and Modifications:
The 1st, 5th, and 9th Dwads in Leo accentuate the Fire Element.
The 1st, 4th, 7th, and 10th Dwads in Leo accentuate the Fixed Quality.
The 1st Dwad in Leo accentuates the solar Disposition.
The 3rd, 6th, 9th, and 12th Dwads in Leo (correspond to Cardinal Signs) and the 2nd, 5th, 8th, and 11th Dwads in Leo (correspond to Mutable Signs) show perhaps less emphasis on Fixity.
The 6th and 7th Dwads in Leo are somewhat saturnian, not so typically solar.
The Dwads do not change the nature of the Sign; they accentuate and modify the interpretation. All of Leo is leonian.

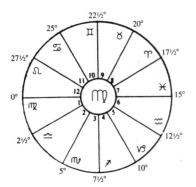

THE SIGN VIRGO

Element: Earth
Quality: Mutable
Disposition: mercurial
Ruler: Mercury

Virgo contains 30°
It is divided into 12 Dwads
Each Dwad contains 2½°

Fig. 10. The Wheel and Zodiac in Virgo

Table 15
Sign Virgo

Dwad-House*	Dwad-Sign**	Quality & Element of Dwad-Sign		"Sub-ruler"
1st	Virgo	Mutable	Earth	Mercury
2nd	Libra	Cardinal	Air	Venus
3rd	Scorpio	Fixed	Water	Mars
4th	Sagittarius	Mutable	Fire	Jupiter
5th	Capricorn	Cardinal	Earth	Saturn
6th	Aquarius	Fixed	Air	Saturn & Uranus
7th	Pisces	Mutable	Water	Jupiter & Neptune
8th	Aries	Cardinal	Fire	Mars (& Pluto)
9th	Taurus	Fixed	Earth	Venus
10th	Gemini	Mutable	Air	Mercury
11th	Cancer	Cardinal	Water	Moon (& Earth)
12th	Leo	Fixed	Fire	Sun

* Each Dwad-House corresponds to the House which has the same Number.
**Each Dwad-Sign corresponds to the Sign which has the same Name.
Some Accentuations and Modifications:
The 1st, 5th, and 9th Dwads in Virgo accentuate the Earth Element.
The 1st, 4th, 7th, and 10th Dwads in Virgo accentuate the Mutable Quality.
The 1st and 10th Dwads in Virgo accentuate the mercurial Disposition.
The 3rd, 6th, 9th, and 12th Dwads in Virgo show a "tinge of Fixity."
The 4th and 7th Dwads in Virgo are somewhat jovial.
The Dwads do not change the nature of the Sign; they accentuate and modify the interpretation. All of Virgo is virgoan.

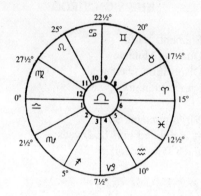

THE SIGN LIBRA

Element: Air
Quality: Cardinal
Disposition: venusian
Ruler: Venus

Libra contains 30°
It is divided into 12 Dwads
Each Dwad contains 2½°

Fig. 11. The Wheel and Zodiac in Libra

Table 16
Sign Libra

Dwad-House*	Dwad-Sign**	Quality & Element of Dwad-Sign		"Sub-ruler"
1st	Libra	Cardinal	Air	Venus
2nd	Scorpio	Fixed	Water	Mars
3rd	Sagittarius	Mutable	Fire	Jupiter
4th	Capricorn	Cardinal	Earth	Saturn
5th	Aquarius	Fixed	Air	Saturn & Uranus
6th	Pisces	Mutable	Water	Jupiter & Neptune
7th	Aries	Cardinal	Fire	Mars (& Pluto)
8th	Taurus	Fixed	Earth	Venus
9th	Gemini	Mutable	Air	Mercury
10th	Cancer	Cardinal	Water	Moon (& Earth)
11th	Leo	Fixed	Fire	Sun
12th	Virgo	Mutable	Earth	Mercury

* Each Dwad-House corresponds to the House which has the same Number.
**Each Dwad-Sign corresponds to the Sign which has the same Name.
Some Accentuations and Modifications:
The 1st, 5th, and 9th Dwads in Libra accentuate the Air Element.
The 1st, 4th, 7th, and 10th Dwads in Libra accentuate the Cardinal Quality.
The 1st and 8th Dwads in Libra accentuate the venusian Disposition.
The 2nd, 5th, 8th, and 11th Dwads in Libra show a "tinge of Fixity."
The 2nd and 7th Dwads in Libra are somewhat martial, not so typically venusian.
The Dwads do not change the nature of the Sign; they accentuate and modify the interpretation. All of Libra is libran.

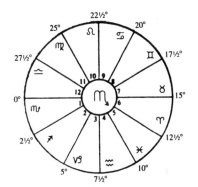

THE SIGN SCORPIO

Element: Water
Quality: Fixed
Disposition: martial
Ruler: Mars (some give Pluto as co-ruler)

Scorpio contains 30°
It is divided into 12 Dwads
Each Dwad contains 2½°

Fig. 12. The Wheel and Zodiac in Scorpio

Table 17
Sign Scorpio

Dwad-House*	Dwad-Sign**	Quality & Element of Dwad-Sign		"Sub-ruler"
1st	Scorpio	Fixed	Water	Mars
2nd	Sagittarius	Mutable	Fire	Jupiter
3rd	Capricorn	Cardinal	Earth	Saturn
4th	Aquarius	Fixed	Air	Saturn & Uranus
5th	Pisces	Mutable	Water	Jupiter & Neptune
6th	Aries	Cardinal	Fire	Mars (& Pluto)
7th	Taurus	Fixed	Earth	Venus
8th	Gemini	Mutable	Air	Mercury
9th	Cancer	Cardinal	Water	Moon (& Earth)
10th	Leo	Fixed	Fire	Sun
11th	Virgo	Mutable	Earth	Mercury
12th	Libra	Cardinal	Air	Venus

* Each Dwad-House corresponds to the House which has the same Number.
**Each Dwad-Sign corresponds to the Sign which has the same Name.
Some Accentuations and Modifications:
The 1st, 5th, and 9th Dwads in Scorpio accentuate the Water Element.
The 1st, 4th, 7th, and 10th Dwads in Scorpio accentuate the Fixed Quality.
The 1st and 6th Dwads in Scorpio accentuate the martial Disposition.
The 3rd, 6th, 9th, and 12th Dwads in Scorpio (correspond to the Cardinal Signs) and the 2nd, 5th, 8th, and 11th Dwads in Scorpio (correspond to Mutable Signs) may indicate more flexibility.
The 7th and 12th Dwads in Scorpio are somewhat venusian, not so typically martial.
The Dwads do not change the nature of the Sign; they accentuate and modify the interpretation. All of Scorpio is scorpionic.

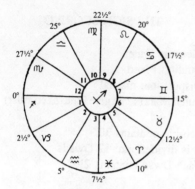

THE SIGN SAGITTARIUS

Element: Fire
Quality: Mutable
Disposition: jovial
Ruler: Jupiter

Sagittarius contains 30°
It is divided into 12 Dwads
Each Dwad contains 2½°

Fig. 13. The Wheel and Zodiac in Sagittarius

Table 18
Sign Sagittarius

Dwad-House*	Dwad-Sign**	Quality & Element of Dwad-Sign		"Sub-ruler"
1st	Sagittarius	Mutable	Fire	Jupiter
2nd	Capricorn	Cardinal	Earth	Saturn
3rd	Aquarius	Fixed	Air	Saturn & Uranus
4th	Pisces	Mutable	Water	Jupiter & Neptune
5th	Aries	Cardinal	Fire	Mars (& Pluto)
6th	Taurus	Fixed	Earth	Venus
7th	Gemini	Mutable	Air	Mercury
8th	Cancer	Cardinal	Water	Moon (& Earth)
9th	Leo	Fixed	Fire	Sun
10th	Virgo	Mutable	Earth	Mercury
11th	Libra	Cardinal	Air	Venus
12th	Scorpio	Fixed	Water	Mars

* Each Dwad-House corresponds to the House which has the same Number.
**Each Dwad-Sign corresponds to the Sign which has the same Name.
Some Accentuations and Modifications:
The 1st, 5th, and 9th Dwads in Sagittarius accentuate the Fire Element.
The 1st, 4th, 7th, and 10th Dwads in Sagittarius accentuate the Mutable Quality.
The 1st and 4th Dwads in Sagittarius accentuate the jupiterian Disposition.
The 3rd, 6th, 9th, and 12th Dwads in Sagittarius show a "tinge of Fixity."
The 7th and 10th Dwads in Sagittarius are somewhat mercurial, not so typically jupiterian.
The Dwads do not change the nature of the Sign; they accentuate and modify the interpretation. All of Sagittarius is sagittarian.

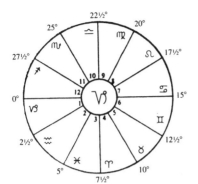

THE SIGN CAPRICORN

Element: Earth
Quality: Cardinal
Disposition: saturnine
Ruler: Saturn

Capricorn contains 30°
It is divided into 12 Dwads
Each Dwad contains 2½°

Fig. 14. The Wheel and Zodiac in Capricorn

Table 19
Sign Capricorn

Dwad-House*	Dwad-Sign**	Quality & Element of Dwad-Sign		"Sub-ruler"
1st	Capricorn	Cardinal	Earth	Saturn
2nd	Aquarius	Fixed	Air	Saturn & Uranus
3rd	Pisces	Mutable	Water	Jupiter & Neptune
4th	Aries	Cardinal	Fire	Mars (& Pluto)
5th	Taurus	Fixed	Earth	Venus
6th	Gemini	Mutable	Air	Mercury
7th	Cancer	Cardinal	Water	Moon (& Earth)
8th	Leo	Fixed	Fire	Sun
9th	Virgo	Mutable	Earth	Mercury
10th	Libra	Cardinal	Air	Venus
11th	Scorpio	Fixed	Water	Mars
12th	Sagittarius	Mutable	Fire	Jupiter

* Each Dwad-House corresponds to the House which has the same Number.
**Each Dwad-Sign corresponds to the Sign which has the same Name.
Some Accentuations and Modifications:
The 1st, 5th, and 9th Dwads in Capricorn accentuate the Earth Element.
The 1st, 4th, 7th, and 10th Dwads in Capricorn accentuate the Cardinal Quality.
The 1st and 2nd Dwads in Capricorn accentuate the saturnine Disposition.
The 2nd, 5th, 8th, and 11th Dwads in Capricorn show a "tinge of Fixity."
The 7th Dwad in Capricorn is somewhat lunar and the 8th Dwad of Capricorn is somewhat solar; so they are not so typically saturnine.
The Dwads do not change the nature of the Sign; they accentuate and modify the interpretation. All of Capricorn is capricornian.

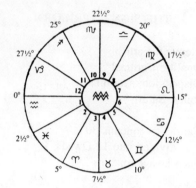

Element: Air
Quality: Fixed
Disposition: saturnine & uranian
Co-rulers: Saturn & Uranus

Aquarius contains 30°
It is divided into 12 Dwads
Each Dwad contains 2½°

Fig. 15. The Wheel and Zodiac in Aquarius

Table 20
Sign Aquarius

Dwad-House*	Dwad-Sign**	Quality & Element of Dwad-Sign		"Sub-ruler"
1st	Aquarius	Fixed	Air	Saturn & Uranus
2nd	Pisces	Mutable	Water	Jupiter & Neptune
3rd	Aries	Cardinal	Fire	Mars (& Pluto)
4th	Taurus	Fixed	Earth	Venus
5th	Gemini	Mutable	Air	Mercury
6th	Cancer	Cardinal	Water	Moon (& Earth)
7th	Leo	Fixed	Fire	Sun
8th	Virgo	Mutable	Earth	Mercury
9th	Libra	Cardinal	Air	Venus
10th	Scorpio	Fixed	Water	Mars
11th	Sagittarius	Mutable	Fire	Jupiter
12th	Capricorn	Cardinal	Earth	Saturn

* Each Dwad-House corresponds to the House which has the same Number.
**Each Dwad-Sign corresponds to the Sign which has the same Name.
Some Accentuations and Modifications:
The 1st, 5th, and 9th Dwads in Aquarius accentuate the Air Element.
The 1st, 4th, 7th, and 10th Dwads in Aquarius accentuate the Fixed Quality.
The 1st and 12th Dwads in Aquarius accentuate the saturnine Disposition.
The 1st Dwad in Aquarius accentuates the uranian Disposition.
The 2nd, 5th, 8th, and 11th Dwads in Aquarius (correspond to the Mutable Quality) and the 3rd, 6th, 9th, and 12th Dwads in Aquarius (correspond to the Cardinal Quality) show more flexibility.
The 6th Dwad in Aquarius is somewhat lunar and the 7th Dwad in Aquarius is somewhat solar; so these two Dwads are not quite so typically saturnine-uranian.
The Dwads do not change the nature of the Sign; they accentuate and modify the interpretation. All of Aquarius is aquarian.

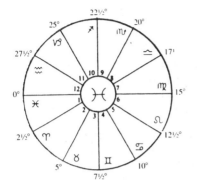

THE SIGN PISCES

Element: Water
Quality: Mutable
Disposition: jupiterian & neptunian
Co-rulers: Jupiter & Neptune

Pisces contains 30°
It is divided into 12 Dwads
Each Dwad contains 2½°

Fig. 16. The Wheel and Zodiac in Pisces

Table 21
Sign Pisces

Dwad-House*	Dwad-Sign**	Quality & Element of Dwad-Sign		"Sub-ruler"
1st	Pisces	Mutable	Water	Jupiter & Neptune
2nd	Aries	Cardinal	Fire	Mars (& Pluto)
3rd	Taurus	Fixed	Earth	Venus
4th	Gemini	Mutable	Air	Mercury
5th	Cancer	Cardinal	Water	Moon (& Earth)
6th	Leo	Fixed	Fire	Sun
7th	Virgo	Mutable	Earth	Mercury
8th	Libra	Cardinal	Air	Venus
9th	Scorpio	Fixed	Water	Mars
10th	Sagittarius	Mutable	Fire	Jupiter
11th	Capricorn	Cardinal	Earth	Saturn
12th	Aquarius	Fixed	Air	Saturn & Uranus

* Each Dwad-House corresponds to the House which has the same Number.
**Each Dwad-Sign corresponds to the Sign which has the same Name.
Some Accentuations and Modifications:
The 1st, 5th, and 9th Dwads in Pisces accentuate the Water Element.
The 1st, 4th, 7th, and 10th Dwads in Pisces accentuate the Mutable Quality.
The 1st and 10th Dwads in Pisces accentuate the jupiterian Disposition.
The 1st Dwad in Pisces accentuates the neptunian Disposition.
The 3rd, 6th, 9th, and 12th Dwads in Pisces show a "tinge of Fixity."
The 4th and 7th Dwads in Pisces are somewhat mercurial, so not so typically jupiterian/neptune.
The Dwads do not change the nature of the Sign; they accentuate and modify the interpretation. All of Pisces is piscean.

The Wheel within Each Sign

In each Sign of 30° there are, so to speak, 12 "Dwad-Houses," each of which contains 02° 30'.

42

Table 22
Some Meanings of the 12 Dwad-Houses within Each Sign

Begins at:	Dwad-House:
00° 00′ 00″	1st: Personal interests and own efforts.
02° 30′ 00″	2nd: Values; personal resources and talents; income.
05° 00′ 00″	3rd: Mental interests: communication, exchange of ideas.
07° 30′ 00″	4th: Fundamentals; "roots"; finalities and conclusions.
10° 00′ 00″	5th: Creativity, self-expression; heart interests; recreation.
12° 30′ 00″	6th: Service; adjustments; selectivity and assimilation.
15° 00′ 00″	7th: Reaction; relatedness; "open" cooperation or opposition.
17° 30′ 00″	8th: Intense emotions, sexuality; productivity; transitions; investigation.
20° 00′ 00″	9th: Religion and/or philosophy; abstractions; expansiveness.
22° 30′ 00″	10th: Ambition; mastery; authority and control.
25° 00′ 00″	11th: Knowledge; friendliness; "circumstances."
27° 30′ 00″	12th: The unconscious and unknown, under-currents, "behindscenes."

Note: All of the above meanings are applicable in any kind of Chart ("Flat — Natural Zodiacal Wheel, with Aries in 1st House; Solar Chart, with Sun-Sign in the 1st; Solar-Equilibrium, with Degree of Natal Sun on the Cusp of the 1st House; and the calculated Radix set up for the time and place of birth).

Table 23
Some Meanings of the 12 Dwad-Houses within Each Sign which *may* be used in an *objective* sense in a *Radix Chart* and in *Horary* or *Mundane Astrology*

00° 00′ 00″	1st: Personal appearance, physical body; oneself.
02° 30′ 00″	2nd: Earning power; possessions; tangibles; own assets; money.
05° 00′ 00″	3rd: Neighbor(hood); "brethren"; transportation; written or spoken words; primary education; short trips.
07° 30′ 00″	4th: Estate, housing; home circle; parent or parent substitute.
10° 00′ 00″	5th: Loved ones, children, pets (when like children); avocation.
12° 30′ 00″	6th: Health; food, clothing; daily routine; subordinates such as employees or tenants; chores; small animals; therapy.
15° 00′ 00″	7th: Partner or mate; public; opponent; dealings, transactions, contracts; litigation; contests; "open" encounters.
17° 30′ 00″	8th: Joint assets, mutual benefits; taxes, insurance; outgo; regeneration, transformation; sleep; others' resources.
20° 00′ 00″	9th: Added study (academic or not); *distant* matters or people or travel; future plans; laws; publishing, broadcasting.
22° 30′ 00″	10th: Career, vocation; major projects; status; parent or parent substitute; employer, landlord; achievement; government.
25° 00′ 00″	11th: Friends, acquaintances; associates; advisers; legislators.
27° 30′ 00″	12th: Intangibles; latent talents, hidden assets; privacy, confidential matters; institutions; quiet preparation; concealment, confinement, retreat; large animals.

As you can see, these meanings must be carefully selected; all would not apply in all circumstances. There are many more Key-words and phrases from which an applicable word might be chosen to indicate the "specifics and particulars" by means of the Dwad-Houses. The above list gives some frequently used examples. Because they are so objective, they are to be used in the interpretation of a Radix Chart (when appropriate) but not with a Flat Chart, Solar or Solar-Equilibrium; because these Charts are subjective rather than objective.

More About Dwad-Houses in the Signs

Just as the Houses of a Wheel can be classified into various categories; so may the *Dwad-Houses* within each and every Sign be classified by certain categories.

Table 24
Dwad-Houses Classified

The Category of PERSONAL INTERESTS:

1st Dwad of any Sign (00° 00′ to 02° 30′): Beginnings, current interests; present.
5th Dwad of any Sign (10° 00′ to 12° 30′): Enterprises from personal past; play.
9th Dwad of any Sign (20° 00′ to 22° 30′): Trends and plans re personal future.

The Category of ACHIEVEMENT:

2nd Dwad of any Sign (02° 30′ to 05° 00′): Talents, resources with which to work.
6th Dwad of any Sign (12° 30′ to 15° 00′): How Native adjusts and works it out.
10th Dwad of any Sign (22° 30′ to 25° 00′): How Native masters and achieves.

The Category of RELATEDNESS:

3rd Dwad of any Sign (05° 00′ to 07° 30′): "Kin folk," relatives by blood.
7th Dwad of any Sign (15° 00′ to 17° 30′): Those met; openly for or against.
11th Dwad of any Sign (25° 00′ to 27° 30′): Those known; friends, associates.

The Category of FEELINGS:

4th Dwad of any Sign (07° 30′ to 10° 00′): Familiar feelings; sense of roots.
8th Dwad of any Sign (17° 30′ to 20° 00′): Intense emotion, sex; release.
12th Dwad of any Sign (27° 30′ to 30° 00′): Unconscious undercurrents;
repression.

Table 25
How Native Moves Along Through Life

The PHYSICAL WORLD and How the Native Acts:

1st Dwad of any Sign: Native himself, own actions; wherever he is.
4th Dwad of any Sign: At home or on familiar ground; re end of matters.
7th Dwad of any Sign: In public or openly with others.
10th Dwad of any Sign: In command or regarding authority (wielded or imposed).

The EMOTIONAL WORLD and How the Native Expresses Emotion:

2nd Dwad of any Sign: About what Native has and what he values; tangibly.
5th Dwad of any Sign: About heart interests, loved ones; dramatically.
8th Dwad of any Sign: About intense emotions, transitions; investigatingly.
11th Dwad of any Sign: About friends, associates, circumstances; wishfully.

The MENTAL WORLD and How the Native Thinks:

3rd Dwad of any Sign: The conscious; concretely (reason).
6th Dwad of any Sign: The subconscious; automatically (habit).
9th Dwad of any Sign: The superconscious; abstractly (theory).
12th Dwad of any Sign: The unconscious; imaginatively (fantasy);
intuitively (mystery).

The "Native" is a term much used in old texts on Astrology to indicate the person for whom the Chart was set up according to his (her) time and place of birth.

Don't try to memorize the Key-words and phrases given; but do become, at least, somewhat familiar with the Dwad-Houses in each Sign, just as you are familiar with some of the meanings of the corresponding Houses in a Radix. The above given Key-phrases may be applied to corresponding Houses also. Only a few meanings are given; but these should be enough to present the idea of how they may be used.

Example for Finding Dwads

Below are listed the positions of Bernard Baruch's Natal Planets. Let me suggest that you cover the portion of this page on which the Dwads are given until you have found them for yourself. Use the Table on page 26 or the diagram on page 21. Then check with those given below.

Table 26
Example for Finding Dwads

Natal Planet	Sign Position	Division: Dwad-House*	Dwad-Sign**
Sun	26° Leo 32' 22"	11th	Gemini
Moon	1° Gemini 44'	1st	Gemini
Mercury	17° Virgo 08'	7th	Pisces
Venus	28° Cancer 43'	12th	Gemini
Mars	17° Cancer 16'	7th	Capricorn
Jupiter	21° Gemini 43'	9th	Aquarius
Saturn	21° Sagittarius 58' ℞	9th	Leo
Uranus	24° Cancer 24'	10th	Aries
Neptune	21° Aries 42' ℞	9th	Sagittarius
Pluto	18° Taurus 47' ℞	8th	Sagittarius
When the Radix Ascendant is known, it and the Part of Fortune are included:			
Radix Asc.	11° Sagittarius 05'	5th	Aries
Fortuna	16° Virgo 17'	7th	Pisces
When the *True* Nodes of the Moon are known, they are included:			
North Node	19° Cancer 11'	8th	Aquarius
South Node	19° Capricorn 07'	8th	Leo

(Note the differences: The Mean Nodes of the Moon are 17° 09' of Cancer and Capricorn, respectively. This is an example of how the *True* Nodes of the Moon are in different Dwads from those apparently occupied. This is the reason why Leipert did not use the Dwads of the Node unless *True* Nodal positions were available. Be sure to use them instead of the Mean North Node given in the Ephemeris, with the South Node opposite.)

* The 12 Divisions of each Sign Leipert called *"The Wheel within each Sign."* Each Division of 02° 30' may be likened to the corresponding House. This can add tremendously to your ability to interpret positions of Planets, not only in Natal Charts, but Transits, Horary, and Mundane Charts.

Each *House* is a Department of Life, a State of Consciousness, and — in the Calculated Radix which shows the actual world of experience — Circumstances and Situations, Conditions, Persons, Places, Things, etc.

Consequently, a Natal Planet's placement in a Dwad can be likened to its occupancy of the corresponding House! (More about this on the next page.)

**The 12 Dwads of each Sign Leipert called *"The Zodiac within each Sign."* Each Dwad of 02° 30' may be likened to the corresponding Sign. *Signs* describe and characterize. *Dwads* (when likened to the corresponding Signs) also characterize and describe, *modifying* the overall description of the Sign itself.

Outline: Natal Planets in Dwad-*Signs*

By following this step by step procedure, you can interrelate the Natal Planets according to their Dwad-*Sign* placements.

STEP ONE:

I — Make list of Natal Planets in the Dwad-*Signs*.

This list of Mr. Baruch's Natal Planets is on page 45. For the present ignore the list of Dwad-Houses (already considered) but copy the list at the extreme right, headed "Dwad-Sign"**. Leipert called them Dwad-*Signs* to contrast them easily with the Dwad-Houses. (You'll probably prefer to list the written symbols instead of the words used in the list.)

⊙ Sun (Planet)   ♊ Gemini (Dwad-*Sign*)

☽ Moon   ♊ Gemini   (etc.)

II — Make a list of the 12 Dwad-*Signs*, beginning with Aries; so you can very easily see which Dwad-*Signs* are occupied by Natal Planets. At this point we are not concerned about which actual Sign the Planets are in, just Dwad-Signs.

Mr. Baruch has one Natal Planet in the Aries Dwad-Sign; none in Taurus Dwad-Sign; in the Gemini Dwad-Sign Sun, Moon, and Venus. Continue on.

1 — Now scan your list of Dwad-Signs to see which are emphasized.

One Natal Planet gives an important Focus.

Two Natal Planets emphasize the Dwad-Signs even more.

Three (or more) Natal Planets in Dwad-Signs of the same name, not necessarily in the same Sign, show a powerful emphasis on the nature of that Dwad-Sign.

Mr. Baruch's Natal Planets show this powerful emphasis on the Gemini Dwad-Signs. Three Natal Planets occupy Gemini Dwad-Signs.

III — Use the same list you made in Step II above, if you left enough space to add the number of the Dwad-House and the symbol for the Sign itself; or:

Make another list, beginning with the Aries Dwad-Sign, showing the numbered Dwad-House and the actual Sign occupied:

This list for Mr. Baruch would begin this way:

Dwad-*Sign* = Dwad-*House* of Sign occupied by Natal Planet:

Aries   = 10th   Cancer occupied by Uranus

Just omit Taurus Dwads-Sign as it is not occupied)

Gemini = 1st   Gemini occupied by Moon

Gemini = 11th   Leo occupied by Sun

Gemini = 12th   Cancer occupied by Venus

Leo   = 9th   Sagittarius occupied by Saturn

etc.

This way it is obvious that the Natal Planets in the Gemini Dwad-Signs, Dwad-Signs which carry the same "name," occupy three different Signs. Therefore, each of these Gemini Dwad-Signs corresponds to a different Dwad-House.

The Focuses of his Natal Moon, Sun, and Venus will be similarly characterized (all described by Gemini Dwad-Signs) yet differently interpreted because each Dwad-House is different.

Ordinarily you would not make this STEP ONE in three stages as shown above. It was presented in this way so you would participate.

Natal Planets in Dwad-Houses

I referred to page 45 to see which Dwad-Houses are occupied by Mr. Baruch's Natal Planets. For the time being we shall ignore the actual Sign positions; we are now interested in Dwad-Houses only.

I scanned the list of Dwad-Houses listed under "Division of Sign," page 45 finding:

Table 27
Natal Planets in Dwad-Houses

1st Dwad-House of some Sign (at this point we aren't concerned about *which* Sign) Natal Moon;

2nd, 3rd, 4th, 5th, and 6th Dwad-Houses: not occupied by any Natal Planet;

7th Dwad-House: (these 7th Dwads are in two Signs, but we are ignoring Signs): Natal Mercury and Natal Mars;

8th Dwad-House: Natal Pluto;

9th Dwad-House: Natal Jupiter, Saturn, and Neptune (each in a different Sign);

10th Dwad-House: Natal Uranus;

11th Dwad-House: Natal Sun and Earth (always in same Dwad-House)

12th Dwad-House: Natal Venus.

While actually interpreting a Chart I combine several of these "steps," taking into consideration the Dwad-Sign as well as the Dwad-House, the Sign itself that is occupied, and the Radix House also, when the time and place of birth are known.

However, the use of the Dwads will be made much clearer if we go one step at a time. Consequently, we are thinking, now, of Planets in Dwad-Houses.

If we compare the above-given Planets in the Dwad-Houses with the Houses occupied in the calculated Radix (not necessarily yet) we'd find that not one of his Natal Planets occupies the Radix Hosue which corresponds to its

Dwad-House. Whenever you do find a Natal Planet in the same Radix House that corresponds to the same-numbered Dwad-House, there is a strong emphasis on the Planet and the House.

The Moon does not rule Mr. Baruch's Rising Sign (Radix Ascendant) nor is it in Radix I. Nevertheless, because it is in the 1st Dwad-House, the Moon should be considered in relation to his "personal interests and own efforts" (see page 42 — list of some Key-words for Dwad-Houses).

His MOON in a 1st Dwad-House shows he is in close personal touch with INSTINCTS in regard to his personal affairs; with SENSITIVITY and RESPONSIVENESS emphasized, especially in matters of personal interest and own efforts, current affairs, etc.

No Natal Planet in a Dwad-House

This does not mean that there is something missing! It merely shows that less *FOCUS* occurs there. Each Dwad may be called a "Focus" on "specifics and particulars."

One or More Natal Planets in a Dwad-House

Just one Natal Planet in a Dwad-House shows Focus on whatever is meant by that Dwad-House.

PLUTO in the 8th Dwad-House: ORGANIZATION, INTEGRATION OF MANY FACTORS, perhaps COMPLEXITY regarding mutual benefits in a productive way.

URANUS in the 10th Dwad-House: INSIGHTS regarding government or management; INDEPENDENCE re authority; INGENUITY in matters of business or career, etc.

SUN in 11th Dwad-House shows the VITAL IMPORTANCE of friendships and associations, to whom and from whom advice might be given; he would wishfully WILL TO BE AND TO DO that which BRIGHTENS the circumstances, in which he is the CENTER.

VENUS is in the 12th of the Dwad-Houses: APPRECIATION of the intangibles, latent talents, hidden assets, etc.

Two or More Natal Planets in a Dwad-House

His MERCURY and MARS occupy the 7th Dwad-House. Please note: they are not in the same zodiacal Sign, nor do they occupy the same House in the Radix. Nevertheless, apart from their being in very close Aspect (actually a Sextile), both these Planets focus in a "7th House manner" because they both occupy the 7th Dwad-House.

MERCURY here shows: Focus on COMMUNICATION with mate, partner, or public; NEWS and RUMORS focused on his transactions, buying, selling, etc.; ATTENTION on public affairs, relationships.

MARS here: ZEAL and EXERTION in dealings with others or in competition; also VALOR in contests; ENERGETIC ACTIVITY in cooperation, etc.

In the 9th House-Dwad there is considerable emphasis because of the Focusing of three Natal Planets therein: JUPITER, SATURN, and NEPTUNE, each in a different zodiacal Sign.

JUPITER in the 9th Dwad-House: FORESIGHT regarding future trends; OPTIMISM in making future plans; likelihood of PROFIT through travel, distant or foreign matters; JUPITER in the 9th Dwad-House is similar to JUPITER in House IX or in the 9th Sign Sagittarius; it is not identical. In the 9th Dwad-House it has a Focus which gives a greater emphasis to it.

Along with the OPTIMISM (JUPITER) he focuses on PRUDENCE and CAUTION regarding plans for the future; SATURN occupies the 9th Dwad-House: PAST EXPERIENCE considered in looking ahead; DISCRETION in expansion or extension. SATURN shows TRADITION in religion or philosophy.

NEPTUNE also is in the 9th Dwad-House: INTUITION regarding future trends; an element of MYSTICISM in religion and philosophy, etc.

Do you see how to blend some "appropriate" Key-words of PLANETS with those of the Dwad-Houses? These are just hints.

Three — or More — Natal Planets in the Same Dwad-House

If three or more Natal Planets occupy the same Dwad-House, there is an outstanding emphasis on this Focus which warrants much attention in your interpretation.

Planets in Square or Opposition Aspect which occupy the same Dwad-House are harmonized to a great extent by their being closely linked together in this way.

* * * * * *

In the Spring of 1936 Carl Leipert taught me this, his way of interpreting Planets in Dwad-Houses. During these many years of my own personal experience with the Dwad-Houses I have noted some interesting examples which I'd like to share with you.

Some Observations

In quite a number of instances Natal JUPITER and SATURN in the same numbered Dwad, that is, the same Dwad-Houses have shown a FLAIR FOR TIMING.

In the 1st Dwad-House: a natural FLAIR FOR TIMING re personal interests and some kind of personal RHYTHM.

In the 2nd Dwad-House: the FLAIR FOR TIMING has to do with talents or assets.

In the 4th Dwad-House: the FLAIR FOR TIMING seems to be particularly related to estate matters, holdings, when to bring things to a close, etc.

These have been effective, more or less, even when the Planets were not especially emphasized obviously in the actual Chart.

Years ago I was much interested in the Rectification of an approximate time of birth and finding a Speculative Radix when the time is not known. Either procedure may be made easier by the use of the Dwad-Houses. The Moon's travel each day through a number of Dwad-Houses permits your trying out of the various ones which could possibly be occupied during the leeway of time. Although it's not conclusive, it may well give a good clue for a start. Other Planets which change Dwads on the date of birth may be used in a similar manner. Try them!

Next, we'll study the Focuses of the Natal Planets shown by their occupancy of the Dwad-Signs.

The Zodiac within Each Sign

Not only does each 2½° Division of each Sign correspond to a House of a Wheel, each one corresponds to a Sign of the Zodiac. We already know something about the interpretation of Natal Planets in Dwad-Houses.

Now we look into Dwad-Signs. Each Dwad-Sign corresponds to the zodiacal Sign which has the same name. Each Dwad-Sign is a Focus which shows specifics and particulars within the Sign itself.

Mr. Baruch's Natal Planets in the Dwad-Signs

The last column on page 45 lists his Natal Planets in the Dwad-Signs. Ignoring the Dwad-Houses, in order to take the second step, we look for Focuses in the Dwad-Signs.

URANUS is the only one in the Aries Dwad-Sign.

SATURN is the only one in the Leo Dwad-Sign.

MARS is the only one in the Capricorn Dwad-Sign.

JUPITER is alone in the Aquarius Dwad-Sign.

MERCURY alone in Pisces Dwad-Sign.

Just one Natal Planet in any Dwad-Sign greatly emphasizes the Focus that should be described by Key-words and phrases for the Dwad-Sign.

Rather than spend time and take up space here, I shall go on to the Dwad-Signs occupied by more than one Natal Planet, feeling that the way to interpret will be clear as we continue. Then you should come back to the above given Planets to interpret them for yourself.

Two of his Natal Planets, NEPTUNE and PLUTO occupy Sagittarius Dwad-Signs, one in the Sign Aries, the other in the Sign Taurus. Both (in fact, all) Sagittarian Dwan-Signs are theoretical, conjecturing, expansive, speculative, seeking and questing, etc. (all Key-words for this Dwad-Sign). The Focuses in the two are described in similar ways, using the same Key-words, only for the Dwad-Signs. However, each of these two is in a different Dwad-House, the former is the 9th of the Sign Aries, while the latter is the 8th of the Sign Taurus. Consequently, the interpretations must differ. (The Earth, also, is in the Sagittarian Dwad-Sign of Aquarius.)

NEPTUNE is in the Sagittarius Dwad-Sign which is the 9th Dwad-House of the Sign Aries. What might this mean? His CREATIVE IMAGINATION is daring and irrepressible (Sign Aries). It is focused in a revealing foresighted way (Sagittarius Dwad-Sign) in regard to future trends and long-range plans (9th Dwad-House). I chose Key-words that are appropriate for CREATIVE IMAGINATION. Other Key-words would have been selected, had I used, say, IDEALISM or INTUITION, etc. for NEPTUNE.

PLUTO is in the Sagittarius Dwad-Sign which is the 8th Dwad-House of the zodical Sign Taurus. His GROUP ACTIVITIES, ORGANIZATIONAL and/or REORGANIZATION ACTIVITIES are worthwhile and valued, perhaps acquisitive (Sign Taurus). They are focused in a wide-spread, long-range, planned ahead way (Sagittarius Dwad-Sign) regarding mutual benefits, joint assets, etc. and perhaps, exchanges. These are Key-words for the 8th Dwad-House that would be appropriately used for GROUP or ORGANIZATIONAL and REORGANIZATIONAL ACTIVITIES.

The above similarities and contrasts of the Neptune and Pluto placements in Sagittarius Dwads to two different zodiacal Signs with their consequently different Dwad-Houses should help you with your own interpretation.

Don't make too much of an effort to memorize Key-words and phrases; instead you should become acquainted with the natures of the Planets, Signs, and Houses; at the same time you are becoming acquainted with the Dwad-Signs and Dwad-Houses.

Three — or More — Natal Planets in the Same Dwad-Sign

This makes for a very outstanding emphasis on the Focus described by the appropriate Key-words. Mr. Baruch has three such Planets. They are not the same one which occupied the same Dwad-House.

Jupiter, Saturn, and Neptune were in the same Dwad-House, the 9th, Focus.

Sun, Moon, and Venus are the three in the same Dwad-Sign, Gemini, Focus.

Note: For clearer interpretation use Key-words and Key-phrases for Dwad-Signs as descriptions; use Key-words and Key-phrases for Dwad-Houses to indicate persons, places, things (who or whom, where and what), etc.

Mr. Baruch's Sun, Moon, and Venus in the Gemini Dwad-Sign

Each occupies a different Sign of the Zodiac. Nevertheless, each has a Focus of a Gemini nature. The Gemini Dwad within each Sign has Gemini characteristics, characteristics which modify the general characteristics of the actual Sign itself. Furthermore, the Dwad indicates particulars and specifics; it pinpoints outstanding features.

His SUN, MOON, and VENUS occupy Gemini Dwad-Signs, one in the Sign Leo, in the Sign Gemini, and in the Sign Cancer, respectively. All Gemini Dwad-Signs (regardless of the Signs occupied) are communicative, diversified, simultaneous, manipualting, adroit, probably alert and informed, etc. (all Key-words for this Gemini Dwad-Sign). The Focuses, therefore, are described in a very similar way, by the use of the appropriate Key-words.

But, because each pertains to a different Dwad-House, these Focuses are different. How do they differ? The Dwad-Houses aren't the same; so their interpretations must be different.

The SUN is in the Gemini Dwad-Sign which is the 11th Dwad-House of the Sign Leo. His is an INNATE ABILITY to be creative, dramatic, dynamic, direct, loyal, (Leo itself, the Sign). This INNATE ABILITY is focused in an adaptable, convenient, mental, somewhat impersonal way (Gemini Dwad-Sign) in regard to friends and associates as well as circumstances in relation to his hopes and wishes (11th Dwad-House).

This interpretation could be greatly amplified; but this gives the idea.

His MOON is in the Gemini Dwad-Sign, the 1st Dwad-House, of the Sign Gemini: a double emphasis on Gemini. His RECEPTIVITY and MOODS are variable, communicable, and recurring (Gemini Sign). They are focused conveniently and immediately (Gemini Dwad-Sign) on his personal interests and own efforts (1st Dwad-House).

His VENUS is in the Gemini Dwad-Sign, the 12th Dwad-House, of the Sign Cancer. His AFFECTIONS and APPRECIATION are sensitive, remembered, cherishing, and enveloping, perhaps nostalgic (Sign Cancer). They are focused intermittently and recurringly and are communicated (Gemini Dwad-Sign) in privacy, intimacies, etc. We could say his VALUES would be retained tenaciously (Cancer Sign) yet adaptable and made pertinent (Gemini Dwad-Sign) to demands and obligations (12th Dwad-House) and with a reflective SENSE OF MEANING that is alertly attentive (Gemini Dwad-Sign) to hidden factors, intangibles, and the unknown quantity (12th Dwad-House).

By now you should have a clear idea of how to proceed, step by step, with the Natal Planets in the Dwad-Signs and Dwad-Houses of the various Signs. So far, we have not considered the Radix House positions of the Natal Planets; that will come later. Before continuing, why don't you try to apply this use of Dwads to your own Natal Planets? (If you haven't done so already!)

* * * * * * * * * * *

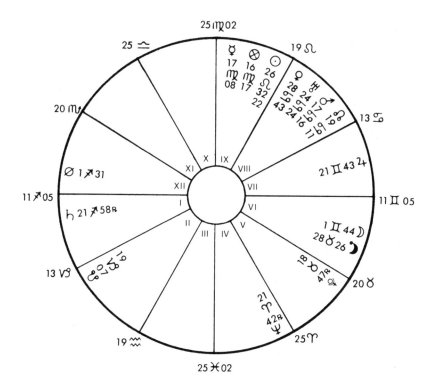

Fig. 17. Bernard Baruch's Radix Chart

Placidian Cusps

Mr. Bernard Baruch
Place of birth: Camden, South Carolina
Latitude: 34° N 14'
Longitude: 80° W 36' = Longitude Time: 5h 22m 24s
Date: 19 August, 1870   "Clock time": 1:50 P.M.
D.S.T.? No   Time: 1:50 P.M. L.M.T. in use
G.M.T.: 7:12 P.M.   Calc. S.T. 11h 41m 43s

54

The birth data was given in *The Sabian Symbols of Astrology* by Marc Edmund Jones. This Radix is used in my *Sidelights of Astrology, The Star Wheel,* and *Essentials of Natal Interpretation with Study Guide* for the benefit of students who wish to follow through with one example. In the Radix on the previous page, however, the *True* Nodes of the Moon are given instead of the Mean or Average Nodes. The Dark Moons, Lilith and Lulu, are included here.

The Houses of the Wheel are States of Consciousness regarding the Departments of Life.

The Radix (both subjective and objective) shows persons, places, and things; it shows circumstances, environment, and the "settings" of Life's drama.

Radix House I is the "window" to the actual world of experience.

Outline: Step Two

Now that we have the Radix available we can incorporate meanings of the Radix Houses into our interpretation of the Focuses indicated by the Dwads.

When the Radix is not available, it is still possible to use the Dwads advantageously, if you keep in mind there is no valid substitute for a calculated Radix which portrays the conditioning and the situations in the actual world.

Step Two: About the Natal Sun

The Natal SUN: the center of consciousness, the sense of identity, volition or the will to be and to do, the vitality, etc.

I — Note the Natal Sun-Sign (the Sign occupied by the Natal SUN).

1 — Describe the above meanings of the SUN by some Key-words for the Sign.

2 — Consider the Element and Quality of the Sun-Sign.

II — Note the Dwad-*Sign* occupied by the Natal SUN.

1 — Using appropriate Key-words for the Dwad-Sign, modify the description of the SUN that was given by the Sign occupied.

2 — Consider the Element and Quality of the Dwad-Sign in this modification.

Be sure to modify the Sun-Sign description by the Dwad-Sign, not vice versa! The Sign predominates; the Dwad-Sign modifies and focuses.

Mr. Baruch's SUN is in the Sign Leo, a Fixed Fire Sign. It is in the Gemini Dwad-Sign (of Leo) which corresponds to Gemini, the Mutable Air Sign.

III — See if any Natal Planets occupy the Sign that corresponds to the Dwad-sign occupied by the Natal SUN. Any such Planet so placed is linked with the SUN.

Mr. Baruch's SUN is in a Gemini Dwad-Sign. Are there any Natal Planets in the Sign Gemini? Yes, Moon and Jupiter.

1 — What is the Radix House occupied by such a Planet? That Radix House is emphasized because the Planet in it is "linked up" with the SUN.

His Moon in Gemini is in the Radix House VI, Jupiter in Radix VII.

2 — What if no Natal Planet is in the Sign that corresponds to the SUN'S Dwad? Then find where the corresponding Sign is in the Radix Houses; in that Department of Life he is able to be more himself than in some areas.

IV — Note the Dispositor of the SUN (the Ruler of the Sign in which the Natal SUN is placed). Now see which Planet rules the Dwad-Sign occupied by the SUN; it is a kind of "Sub-Dispositor," giving a slight tinge of its coloring to the Disposition of the SUN. In case two Planets co-rule the Sign which corresponds: use both as subordinate Co-Dispositors of the SUN.

Mercury is Ruler of Gemini, the corresponding Sign to his SUN'S Dwad-Sign; so Mercury is a kind of "Sub-Dispositor of his SUN."

1 — In which Radix House is this "Sub-Dispositor"? It is emphasized.

His Mercury (Sub-Dispositor of the SUN) emphasizes Radix IX.

V — Note Sign occupied by Natal SUN, the Sun-Sign. There are 12 Dwads (one in each Sign) in the Zodiac which have the name of his own Sun-Sign; all 12 are subtly correlated with the Sun-Sign, having the same name (nature). Are there any Natal Planets in these Dwads (of any Sign)? They are subtly yet closely linked together, whether or not they make Aspects to one another.

Mr. Baruch's Sun is in the Sign Leo. There are 12 Dwads (one in each Sign) that are named Leo Dwad-Signs; all are correlated with the Sign Leo. The only Leo Dwad occupied by a Natal Planet is the Leo Dwad in the Sign Sagittarius, occupied by Saturn. So Saturn is closely linked with his SUN, for more depth, maturity, seriousness, etc. His Sun brightens his Saturn. And the Trine between them is enhanced.

"The Zodiac within Each Sign"

As previously stated, "There is a Zodiac within each Sign."

By dividing the 30° of each zodiacal Sign into twelfths, we obtain 12 Dwads. Each Dwad corresponds to a Sign of the Zodiac, that of the same name.

The corresponding Sign seems to be linked with all the Dwads which are "named" after it. In other words, Key-words and Key-phrases for the corresponding Sign (Table 1) are more or less applicable to all the Dwads of that name. All of the Aries Dwads (one in each Sign), all the Taurus Dwads (one in each Sign) and so on may be somewhat described by Key-words for the Sign Aries and the Sign Taurus, etc., respectively. However, these Key-words do not supersede the Key-words for the Sign of which they form a part! They do not replace the Key-words for the Sign occupied. They add specific and particular description to the description given by the Sign occupied.

Example: Mr. Baruch's Sun 26° Leo 32′ 22″

His Natal Sun is in the Sign Leo. Leo Key-words and phrases are used to characterize and describe his ego, sense of identity, will to be and to do (all indicated by the Sun). His Natal Sun is in the Gemini Dwad of the Sign Leo. The Key-words for the corresponding Sign, Gemini, are more or less applicable in the description of his Natal Sun. However, the Key-words for Gemini must not be so much emphasized as are those of Leo, the Sign occupied by his Sun. There are Gemini specifics and particulars in the Leo interpretation. We could even say, Gemini modifications; but Leo predominates.

Leo is a fixed Fire Sign: purposeful, persevering; enthusiastic, zealous, spontaneous, and intuitive. The Gemini Dwad is linked with the corresponding Sign — Gemini, a mutable Air Sign. Mutable Air will not supersede the fixed Fire, but will modify. Mr. Baruch would be more adaptable, although purposeful and persevering; more impersonal although animated, thinking as well as intuitive.

In contrast:

Suppose the Natal Sun to be in the Sign Gemini, in the Leo Dwad.

Mr. X. could be a "go-between," making connections, adaptable; animated but impersonal and thinking. His Leo Dwad would not really lessen his natural Gemini adaptability but would show it to be more purposeful. He would be communicative (Sign Gemini) in a dramatic or creative way, entertaining, etc. (the Leo Dwad).

We return to Mr. Baruch. His Sun in Leo shows an innate ability to be creative and self-expressive. The Gemini Dwad tends toward a more communicative (verbally or in some dexterous way) kind of self-expression. The Gemini Dwad could also, but not necessarily, show more ability to be manipulative in his investing (Leo). You can continue to develop this combination of Sign and Dwad.

Leipert always placed considerable emphasis on the Natal Sun. He always noted if there were any Natal Planets in the Sign which corresponds to the Dwad of the Natal Sun.

Mr. Baruch's Natal Sun is in a Gemini Dwad; so we look for the corresponding Sign to see if any Natal Planets occupy it. Both the Natal Moon and Jupiter are in Gemini, the corresponding sign to the Dwad occupied by his Sun. These Planets — whether in any Natal Aspect or not to the Natal Sun — seem to be linked with the Sun! This seemed strange to me too, at first; but, over the years, this has proved to be valid.

The Moon means the public, the family, instincts, responses, etc. Jupiter is religion, philosophy, expansiveness, extension, foresight, etc. These would play an important role in relation to Mr. Baruch's will to be and to do. In this example, the Moon and Jupiter are in some Aspects to the Natal Sun anyway; but some link would be there, Aspect or not, because of their being in Gemini.

More on Sign Corresponding to Sun's Dwad

Next, if we wish to extend this kind of linking with the Natal Sun, we note the Radix House positions of the two Planets in Gemini. *Moon is in the Radix House VI,* working conditions, employees, service, adjustments, health, etc. *Jupiter in VII of the Radix,* relationships, the public, buying and selling, dealings, negotiating in personal or other matters, etc. Therefore, Radix Houses VI and VII are given a greater emphasis (in this Dwad Technique) by their being occupied by Natal Planets in Gemini, merely because Gemini is the Sign that corresponds to the Sun's Dwad!

Perhaps you think this is a bit far-fetched. Frankly, that was my first reaction to Leipert's suggestion. If you try this out, I believe you too will be convinced that it is valid.

When There Is No Natal Planet in the Sign which Corresponds to the Dwad Occupied by the Natal Sun

In many instances there is no Natal Planet there; so what is to be done?

Well, the Sign itself does occupy some Radix House. It may be on a Cusp, where it is more obvious. It may be *intercepted* in a Radix House, where it is less obvious but not less important, in the description of the affairs of that department of life. Or it may not be on the Cusp of the House but more than half of this Sign may be within the House (more than 15° of it therein, but not on its Cusp) so it is used to describe, along with the Sign on the Cusp itself.

Suppose that Mr. Baruch's Chart did not have any Natal Planet in Gemini, the Sign corresponding to his Natal Sun's Dwad. Then we would look to the House(s) of the Radix Chart. Approximately 11° Gemini we find on the Cusp of *Radix VII*; so the conditions, circumstances, and opportunities of *relationships, encounters,* his *"public"* (small or great), *dealings, transactions, negotiations,* etc. are areas of significance in relation to his will to be and to do; he identifies well with such situations. We would ignore the part of Gemini in Radix House VI, because the 11° portion of Gemini in House VI is less than half the Sign.

The Radix House(s) occupied by more than half of the Sign, with the Sign intercepted, and above all on the Cusp the Sign which corresponds to the

Dwad occupied by the Natal Sun shows the situations, circumstances, etc. with which you are especially able to identify. Remember, you are especially able to "be yourself" in the area indicated by the Radix House position of the Natal Sun. This is a very meaningful point in your analysis of the Chart.

The Ruler of the Sun's Dwad-Sign

Of course, *always,* the *Ruler* of the *Sign* in which the Sun or Planet is placed, *always* is the Dispositor which gives its Disposition to any and all Natal Planets that occupy the Sign.

The Sun is Dispositor of Planets in Leo; Moon is, for all in Cancer; Mercury is, for all in Gemini and Virgo; Venus is, for all in Taurus and Libra; Mars is, for all in Aries and Scorpio; Jupiter is, for Sagittarius, and Co-Dispositor with Neptune, for all in Pisces; Saturn is, for all in Capricorn, Co-Dispositor with Uranus, for all in Aquarius — regardless of the Dwads occupied. I repeat this; so there will be no confusion about the Dispositors of Planets in the Signs. I use Pluto as Co-Dispositor of Planets in Aries. I use the Earth as Co-Dispositor of Cancer, following Leipert's suggestion.

Leipert did not go so far as to say that the Ruler of the Sun's Dwad should be classified as a "Dispositor" of the Sun, not even a "*Co*-Dispositor"; but, the Ruler of the Dwad (really, the Sign which corresponds to that Dwad) could be called a kind of "*Sub*-Dispositor" of the Sun. It modifies and is a kind of *subordinate,* subordinate to the actual Ruler of the Sign itself.

Keeping in mind that the Sun, Ruler of the Sign Leo, is the Dispositor of his Natal Sun, we look to see which Planet rules the Dwad of Leo occupied by Natal Sun: Natal Sun is in the Gemini Dwad of Leo. Mercury rules Gemini, the corresponding Sign. Therefore, Mercury, to a limited extent, gives its disposition to the Sun in our example.

In which Radix House is Mercury placed? In Radix IX. Radix Houses have to do with the actual world of experience. Now we find an *extra* emphasis on House IX, because the Ruler of the Natal Sun's Dwad is there. There is extra emphasis on his dealing with information in making major decisions regarding longrange planning about his personal future, foreign or distant matters, travel, education, or other meanings of Radix IX. Communication is given an extra emphasis (Mercury).

Frankly, this is not quite so good an example as I would like for this point; Natal Sun is in Radix IX anyway. But it serves to give you the idea of how you give emphasis or *extra* emphasis to the Radix House occupied by the Ruler of that Sign which corresponds to the Sun's Dwad.

To relate all of this to your own Chart — and to any Chart in which you are interested — follow through in a similar way. You may find some subtle, but nonetheless significant interrelationships between and among Planets that are not in Aspect.

Natal Planets in Dwads which Correspond to the Sun-Sign

There does seem to be a subtle, but meaningful, linking together of the Natal Sun and Natal Planets which occupy Dwads which correspond to the Sign occupied by the Sun! This seems to apply whether these particular Planets are in some Aspect with the Natal Sun or not.

Mr. Baruch's Natal Sun is in the Sign Leo. Are there any Natal Planets in the Leo Dwad of any Sign? Yes, Saturn is in the Leo Dwad of the Sign Sagittarius; it is not in the Sign of Leo, but in the *Leo Dwad* of some other Sign. Of course this does not mean that Saturn is to be interpreted as being in the Sign Leo, for it is in Sagittarius. Nevertheless, by virtue of its being in the *Leo Dwad,* Saturn is closely linked with his Natal Sun in the Sign Leo. In this Chart they happen to be in Trine also. But without the Aspect there would still be a close linking together.

Do you personally have any Natal Planets in Dwads which link up with the Sun-Sign? If so, pay extra attention to those Planets and what they mean.

The Importance of the Sun's Dwad

"The Sun is the Essence of the Chart"

Have you been wondering why so much emphasis has been placed on the Natal Sun — its Sign position, the Dwad-Sign occupied, etc.? We checked to see if any of the Natal Planets in the example Chart were in the Sign which corresponds to the Dwad-Sign occupied by the Sun. We emphasized the importance of the "Sub-Dispositor" of the Natal Sun. We looked for Natal Planets in Dwads which have the same name as the Sun-Sign. All of these Planets, subtly linked with the Sun in this Dwad Technique, are of special significance in the analysis of a Chart.

The Sun is the Giver of light and Life; it is the Spark, the Divine Spark, the light of which is reflected to us by all the Planets in our solar system. Each Planet reflects the Light of the Sun in its own way. According to Leipert, each Planet in our solar system (Earth included) has its own vortex; but all the vortices are within the vortex of the Sun itself.

The visible Sun is like a nucleus, the center, the core. We usually limit our concept of the Sun to the incandescent body "out there" in space. We see it rise, culminate, and set, then rise again the next day.

Instead of thinking of the Sun as "out there, apart from us," let us, for the moment at least, shift our view. We are within the vortex of our Sun. Or we can say we are within the aura, the electro-magnetic field of the Sun itself. We are a part of it (not apart from it). No wonder the Sun in the Chart is important! If you think this is a flight of fancy, please bear with us; we'll be back "down to Earth" again shortly!

Notwithstanding the singular importance of the Sun we use Geo-centric (Earth-centererd) Astrology instead of Helio-centric (Sun-centered) Astrology to relate us to Earth. During our life here, Earth is our sphere of activity. To me this is a logical reason why the Tropical Zodiac of Signs is valid. And observation certainly confirms its validity, in planting as well as other ways.

The Dwad occupied by the Natal Sun is like an ever opened "door" of consciousness. Leipert named it the "Golden Door" to imply its radiant entrance to enlightenment. Here is the focus on the ego, the sense of identity, the sense of self; this comes about first. Then comes, through this same "Door" of Consciousness a sensing of more than just the ego. Instead of just the particularized individual, apart from all the other particularized individuals, there comes into conscious being the Individual — in the greater sense of the word — indivisible and inseparable, in the state of Wholeness. Far from its being "inflation," it is the recognition and acceptance of all the factors (conscious and unconscious) of the Psyche.

Leipert was deeply engrossed in the study of the Psyche and the integration of the Total Personality. He called the entire Sun-Sign "the Golden Gate of Consciousness," the Sun's Dwad within that Sign, "the Golden Door" which opens — first to the ego, and then, potentially — to the Self. The precious uniqueness of each one is a facet of the One.

The "Gold" of the Gate and the Door is the Gold of the alchemist. Each one of us (knowingly or not) is engaged in the Work of transforming "base metal into Gold." From Leipert's viewpoint the understanding of the overall potentials that are shown (I nearly wrote "shone" [!] which might be more appropriate here) by the Sun-Sign helps to delineate the ego; the Focus of the Sun's Dwad highlights the portrait. Moreover, the Sun's Dwad is the open "Door" to self-consciousness and thence on to Self-Consciousness.

More About the Natal Sun's Dwad

Let me tell you about Leipert's project relative to the Natal Sun's Dwad. With two volumes of the German Ephemerides (one in each jacket pocket) and his pad of paper for notes he went into many places of business, interviewing those who would answer his questions. First, he asked for the complete date of birth. When given a birthday without the year, he was able to ascertain the Sun's Dwad approximately in most instances. In this project all he sought was the Sun's Dwad. Why that, and nothing else? Because he wanted to see if the Sun's Dwad alone could indicate the individual's Focus on his will to be and do.

Apart from the comparative few who have no need for a job, those who do not follow a business or profession, most of us are more "ourselves" in a vocational or avocational activity than in any other. So Leipert questioned sales people, those at information desks, theater cashiers and ushers, bank managers and clerks, newspaper vendors, policemen, waiters, waitresses, chefs, bar tenders, bus drivers and streetcar conductors, florists, barbers, travel agents, etc. Nearly everyone he asked replied to his questions.

At first, he asked them if they liked their jobs, noting the kind of activity, whether or not it was agreeable, and the Sun's Dwad. Later, he asked the birthdate and then proceeded to tell them whether they were satisfied with the type of job or were working toward some other field or perhaps another phase of the field they were in. Leipert's various pockets provided a file for the noted facts systematically placed in the proper pocket. No, this was not at all ludicrous. Always neatly dressed, scholarly appearing, very polite, even gracious, but very intent on acquiring information, he was seldom rebuffed.

His project resulted in some worthwhile, applicable observations. His purpose had not been to make a statistical survey of the kind of jobs people had in relation to their Sun's positions. He wanted to find out if those who felt they were like "round pegs in square holes" had positions in harmony with their Sun's Dwads.

During his project he made some interesting observations.

Many of the news vendors, reporters, messengers, telegraphers, those at information desks, and quite a few stationers, taxi drivers, and some secretaries emphasized the Sign Gemini, the Decanate Gemini, some Gemini Dwad-Sign, or some 3rd Dwad-House placement of the Natal Sun.

Those who emphasized the Sign Libra, Decanate Libra, some Libra Dwad-Sign (regardless of the Sign itself), or some 7th Dwad-House as the Sun's placement seemed to be especially satisfied in jobs which offered contacts with others.

The Sign Aquarius, an Aquarian Decan, some Aquarian Dwad-Sign or some 11th Dwad-House was almost equally involved with people, perhaps in some advisory or counseling capacity.

The Dwads of Libra and Aquarius nature (in any Sign) and those of the 7th or 11th House nature (in any Sign) were the placements of Natal Suns of those who particularly had the inner urge to deal with people rather than with things.

In our example: Mr. Baruch's Natal Sun occupies an 11th Dwad-House; it is the Gemini Dwad-Sign of the Sign Leo, in the Aries Decan. This combination may well account for his role of adviser; he must have been "very much himself" in the verbal exchange of ideas with his associates and acquaintances.

The Dwad occupied by the Natal Sun does not always show the actual career followed. But when the vocation differs greatly from the nature of the Sun's Dwad a meaningful hobby or avocational activity of that nature can make all the difference in the world in the person's sense of identity and the ability to express himself more fully and creatively, in the job he holds or out of it.

The Dwad Occupied by the Earth

The Natal Earth is always directly opposite the Natal Sun, in the same degree, minute, and second of the Sign opposite the Sun-Sign. These two form a Polarity of great significance.

While the Sun's Dwad is the highlight of greatest Creativity the Dwad occupied by Natal Earth is that of greatest Receptivity; the latter is the area of nourishment, of Mother Earth and all that term implies.

The Golden Door of the Sun is the way to the ego and the Self. The Door of the Earth is to this mundane world and what it offers, also that which we can cultivate to be more at home in this mundane sphere.

Mr. Baruch's Natal Earth is in the 11th Dwad-House, the Sagittarius Dwad-Sign, in the Libra Decan of the Sign Aquarius. The Dwad-House is the same, always, for both Sun and Earth; the Dwad-Signs, Decans, and Signs are always opposites.

His sense of the mundane world is knowledgeable and friendly, yet impersonal (Sign Aquarius). It is focused in a long-range, widespread way by which he plans ahead — Sagittarius Dwad-Sign — regarding hopes and wishes and interests shared with associates and friends. In these areas he is especially receptive and able to orient himself to this mundane existence and what it offers, if he cultivates it and is receptive.

If you wish to go further with the interpretation of the Dwad occupied by his Natal Earth, look to see which Planets (if any) are in Sagittarius Dwad-Signs: Neptune is in the Sagittarius Dwad-Sign of Aries and Pluto in the Sagittarius Dwad-Sign of Taurus. Consequently, Neptune and Pluto are subtly linked with his Earth; although the linking together is "subtle" there is a similarity of Focus. Dwads always denote Focuses. So here is a "triple" Focus of a Sagittarian nature: emphasis on long-range, expansive, far-reaching, directed interests which can — because his Natal Earth occupies this Dwad — be effective in regard to his worldly situation. Neptune indicates his creative imagination and intuition; Pluto, his organizational and group activities.

Try this out in your own Chart; it may be very helpful for your better understanding of how better to focus on this world.

The Dwad of the Radix Ascendant

Include this too when the Radix is available. Sometimes the Dwad will help you to determine the exact Ascendant when there is some doubt about the time of birth.

Mr. Baruch's Ascendant, 11° Sagittarius 05', occupies the Aries Dwad-Sign, the 5th Dwad-House of the Sign Sagittarius, indicating a more forceful, assertive, and energetic (Aries Dwad-Sign) approach to his world of experience shown by the Radix. Radix House I is the most personal part; it is the viewpoint, the window to the actual world of experience; it has much to do with physical appearance and mannerisms, general attitude, etc.

The Sign Aries (corresponding to the Dwad-Sign on his Ascendant) is on the Cusp of Radix V, linking him personally to investments, heart interests, creativity, self-expression, etc. More than half of Aries is in House IV, showing his less obvious (not on the Cusp) interest and activity in holdings, estate matters, family circle, conclusions, etc.

His Natal Uranus occupies an Aries Dwad-Sign; so there is a subtle tinge of Uranian independence and unpredictability about his viewpoint and personal appearance, etc.

The 5th Dwad-House occupied emphasizes his Focus on creativity, self-expression, investments — on all the meanings of the 5th Dwad-House — in a personal, physical way (Radix I).

The more you use the Dwad occupied by the Radix Ascendant in your analysis the more impressive this Dwad Technique becomes. It points out interconnections between and among different factors of the Chart that are not obviously related by Aspect or any other Sign or House placement. It contributes greatly to a comprehensive, in-depth interpretation. Furthermore, it is very simple, after you become familiar with the Dwads.

Dwads Occupied by the True Nodes

The True Nodes of the Moon and Planets

In using the Dwads occupied by the Nodes of the Moon and/or Planets it is essential that the TRUE Nodes be used. The Mean (Average) Nodes of the Moon are always exactly opposite each other. This is not true about the TRUE Nodes. Each Node must be calculated. Refer to TRUE Nodes of the Moon and Planets; J. Allen Jones.

Be sure to copy the Moon's TRUE Nodes into the Chart directly from the book from the date previous to the date of birth. Do not proportion them for your birthday. Each Node remains the same until the next time the Moon (or Planet) again crosses the Ecliptic to go North (the North Node) and South (the South Node). Leipert was most insistent about this after years of careful checking these points.

All the True Nodes are important but those of the Moon are most frequently inserted in the Chart. When a Natal Planet is very close (within about one degree) to a True Node, of itself or of some other Planet, it is wise to note it when a very thorough interpretation is being made.

The True North Node of the Moon or of a Planet is a sensitive Point, indicative of increase, gain, and probably added confidence. It is "in coming."

The True South Node of the Moon or of a Planet is a sensitive Point, indicative of release or letting go, and possibly less confidence. It is "out going" (in the sense of letting go). It is more "automatic" than deliberate.

Mr. Baruch's True North Node of the Moon is in the 8th Dwad-House, the Aquarius Dwad-Sign of Cancer. He is tenacious regarding gains; his innate confidence is focused in a knowing way.

His True South Node of the Moon is also in the 8th Dwad-House (note: the Two True Nodes are not always in the same Dwad-House because they are not always this close to an Opposition). It is in the Leo Dwad-Sign of Capricorn: he can release and "let go" in a creative and dramatic way, perhaps in regard to investing; for this is the Leo Focus of the Sign Capricorn, business-like, ambitious, and authoritative.

Both True Nodes in the 8th Dwad-House focus on mutual benefits and joint assets in which there would be both marked coming in and going out. His Natal Pluto occupies the 8th Dwad-House of a Sign; so there is a linking together of both True Nodes with Pluto, organizational and complex activities.

His True North Node of the Moon is in an Aquarius Dwad-Sign; another of the Aquarius Dwad-Signs is occupied by his Natal Jupiter; so there is a linking together of Jupiter, optimism, with Moon's True North Node, confidence, to make quite a combination.

Interestingly, Saturn, caution, and the Moon's True South Node, frequently indicative of a lack of confidence, are linked together by their being in Leo Dwad-Signs. You could link Saturn with the Moon's South Node: past experience, his own or tradition, might be closely linked with almost automatic letting go.

Natal Venus Conjunct its North Node

On August 18, 1870 (the day just prior to his birth) Venus crossed the Ecliptic into North Latitude; it was conjunct its own True North Node. There is more than one degree of orb, but it is still a valid Conjunction between his Natal Venus with its own True North Node, making for an extra emphasis on its gainful and attracting nature. This accenturates his innate appreciation of the beautiful and his refinement. His Natal Venus occupies the Dwad adjacent to that occupied by its own True North Node. Leipert was accustomed to the allowance of the adjacent Dwad for the orb of such a Conjunction.

Not only is Mr. Baruch's Natal Venus within the next Dwad (adjacent Dwad) to that occupied by Venus at the time of its Conjunction with its own North Node, his Natal Venus has moved only about 06' North in Latitude, as shown by the *Ephemeris* for 1870.

Orbs must be kept very close for Natal Planets in Conjunction with Nodes, whether with their own or with those of other Planets. One degree orb is very powerful; but placement in the adjacent Dwad is also valid for the Conjunction. It is not advisable to increase the Orb beyond the adjacent Dwad for such a Conjunction of a Natal Planet to its own True Node or the True Node of some other Planet.

Leipert did not use other Aspects to the Nodes of the Planets, except when some Planet occupied that sensitive Point; this could be an effective Transit that "set off" the Square (or whatever Aspect was made). The Nodes are sensitive Points; they are not actual bodies. True Nodes mark the Celestial Longitudes where the Planets were when they crossed the Ecliptic; consequently, these are the Points, "sensitive" until another crossing is made by the same Planet in the same direction.

In Example: Natal Venus Conjunct Saturn's North Node

The crossing of the Ecliptic into North Latitude by Saturn had occurred in 1857 at 28° Cancer. This Point is "sensitive" until Saturn's next crossing into North Latitude. The North Node of the Moon or of any Planet is indicative of increase and gain; for Saturn it would be in regard to experience, tradition, carefulness, etc. His Natal Venus is conjunct the True North Node of Saturn in the same Dwad, a 12th Dwad-House, the Gemini Dwad-Sign of Cancer.

Please note: the North Node of Saturn at "23° Cancer 00′" given elsewhere is only a Mean (Average) Node; it is not close enough to the True Node to be properly used. Leipert completely ignored mean Nodes of Planets.

Leipert noted that the North Node of the Moon or Planet should not be called the "good" Node nor should the South Node of the Moon or Planet be called the "bad" Node. He was distressed when people made this classification. Of course, the distinction between them must be clearly made. The North Nodes "bring to" and the South Nodes "take from" or "release." What we should remember is that from time to time it is as desirable to release as to receive. The "receiving" and the "releasing" indicated by the North and South Nodes respectively form a kind of rhythm, each one serving its own purpose. "Release" at the right time, in the right way is certainly not to be considered "bad." From the standpoint of psychological release, the South Nodes of Moon and Planets are significant. Often there is a psychological need where the Moon's South Node is. It may also show "the path of least resistance"; but this need not be entirely negative, not when other parts of the personality and abilities are cultivated and expressed.

Interpretation of Planets and Points in the Radix Houses is not the purpose of this book. Nevertheless, Mr. Baruch's South Node of the Moon in his Radix House II is an excellent example. Here is his need for security (probably more of a psychological than actual need). It shows that at times he would let go of possessions. A means for the releasing of pent-up feelings would be the cultivation and nurtiring of talents which he could almost automatically bring forth. He might automatically adopt the role of "Money man" or "Financier"; this could be a loss in the development of his total personality IF he confined himself to this role only; otherwise, it might be an easy way to meet the outer world.

Dwads Occupied by Lilith and Lulu

Mr. Baruch's Natal Lilith occupies the 1st Dwad-House, the Sagittarius Dwad-Sign of the Sign Sagittarius. There is a seeking, questing, wandering (and wondering!) facet of himself that is IN THE DARK. It is related to his own personal interests and own efforts (LILITH occupies a 1st Dwad-House in the Sign on Radix House I). Not only is LILITH "IN THE DARK," it occupies Radix House XII, House of the unconscious and unknown, latent assets, etc. Religious and philosophical in his view of his actual world of experience (Sagittarius rising) he may well have far more personal interest in such views than he would bring out into the light.

He tends to encounter THE SHADOW (personal and/or collective) in religious and educational fields.

Interestingly, his Natal LULU occupies a 12th Dwad-House, the Aries Dwad-Sign, in the Sign Taurus. It occupies Radix House VI. Here is more emphasis on the unconscious and unknown and his SENSITIVITY (both Lilith and Lulu show a FEELING and SENSING) in regard to latent talents of his subordinates and employees; he would value such latent talents and energetically work with them. The Sign Aries which corresponds to the Dwad-Sign is on the Cusp of Radix House V, relating the Focus (shown by the Dwad) to investments and creativity.

Both Lilith and Lulu seem to be somewhat lunar in nature; but they belong to a shadowy realm. All three have to do with the "night side" of life. LUNA, our visible Moon, reflects the light of the Sun, and is frequently called one of "the Lights."

Perhaps there are more Dark Moons of the Earth. I have read more than once the Earth has had 4 Moons, according to traditions. At the moment the source of that statement escapes me. It would be interesting, wouldn't it? if the Earth does have, along with Luna (the Moon which reflects the light of the Sun) Lilith, and Lulu, still another Dark Moon? To show more components of the Shadow!

Mr. Baruch's Fortuna in the Pisces Dwad in Virgo

With his Fortuna in the 7th Dwad-House this happiness and state of well-being is found in relationships and dealings with others; in a Pisces Dwad-Sign the happiness is not diminished, but there may be a more intimate confidential focus on the detailed and analytical (Virgo) planning ahead (Radix House IX). This could be gone into more fully, of course; but this gives a clue as to how to proceed in the interpretation of Fortuna and any other "Arabian Part" or Sensitive Point in the Radix. The time of birth must be accurate in order to have correct Parts.

"Dwad Wheel"

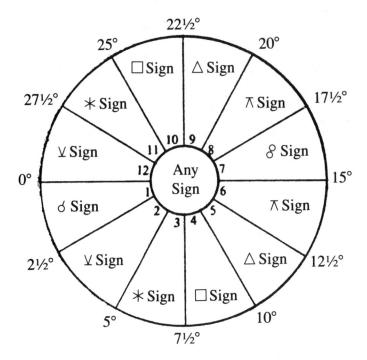

Fig. 18. An Easy Way to Find the Dwads.

What can you do — when you do not have the Table or the Figure of Dwads or the Wheels of Dwads within each Sign at hand — and you'd like to know the Dwad-House and Dwad-Sign a Planet occupies?

Leipert showed me an easy way, an "instant" finder, after just a little practice. This Wheel was given in my *Side Lights of Astrology* on page 28.

Here is the way you use it.

A Sign contains 30°.
A Sign is divided into 12 Dwads.
Each Dwad contains 2½°.

The above Wheel of Dwad-Houses/Dwad-Signs may be used for any Sign.
The figures indicate the Numbers of the Dwad-Houses in any Sign.
Each Dwad-House contains 2½°; each begins with the degree at its "Cusp," as indicated on the above Wheel.

Table 28
An Easy Way to Find the Dwads

The 1st Dwad is given the Name of the Sign itself.

The Names of these Dwad-Signs follow in the order of the Signs.

Each Dwad-Sign corresponds to the Sign with the same Name.

The 1st, 5th, and 9th Dwad-Signs are of the same Element as the Sign itself.

The 1st, 4th, 7th, and 10th Dwad-Signs are of the same Quality as the Sign.

The 1st Dwad-Sign has the Name of the Sign itself, for which the Wheel was made.

The 7th Dwad-Sign has the Name of the Sign opposite the Sign itself.

The 5th and 9th Dwad-Signs correspond to the Signs in Trine to the Sign itself.

The 4th and 10th Dwad-Signs correspond to the Signs in Square to the Sign itself.

The 3rd and 11th Dwad-Signs correspond to the Signs in Sextile to the Sign itself.

The 2nd and 12th Dwad-Signs correspond to the Signs in Semi-Sextile to the Sign.

The 6th and 8th Dwad-Signs correspond to the Signs in Quincunx to the Sign.

Example: Mr. Baruch's Natal Sun is in the Sign Leo; so we apply the Wheel to the Sign Leo. His Sun is at 26° 32' 22" of that Sign. 26° 32' 22" would be in the 11th Dwad-House; the Dwad-Sign is, therefore Gemini which corresponds to the Sign in Sextile to Leo itself. It is Gemini, not Libra (the other Sextile Sign to Leo) because Gemini precedes Leo in the order of the Signs.

His Saturn at 21° 58' Sagittarius is in the 9th Dwad-House of Sagittarius. Now we apply the above Wheel to Sagittarius as the Sign itself. The 9th Dwad-Sign is that which corresponds to a Trine Sign to Sagittarius, Leo.

Since the above Wheel applies to "any" Sign, use it for the Sign occupied by any Planet, Cusp, or Sensitive Point.

Dwads of Longitudinal Parallels

In my *Essentials of Natal Interpretation with Study Guide,* an A.F.A. publication, I devoted a number of pages to the interpretation of the Longitudinal Parallels. In that book we found the Longitudinals from 0° Aries and 0° Libra (the Equinoctial Points) and those from 0° Cancer and 0° Capricorn (the Solstitial Points) in the more usual way. We measured exact distances from the Cardinal Points in degrees and minutes.

Here we measure the distance of the Natal Planet, True Node, Radix Angle or Arabian Part from the nearer Cardinal Point (on each Axis, Equinoctial and Solstitial) in *Dwads* rather than in degrees and minutes.

Admittedly, this method for measuring the distances by Dwads looks far less precise. Nevertheless, it is accurate. This method offers additional clues for detailed interpretation by way of the meanings of the Dwads.

Furthermore, this method is faster than the other way of subtracting the degree and minute of the Natal Planet, True Node, Radix Angle or whatever, from the 30° in each Sign to find the degree and minute where the Longitudinal Parallel occurs.

What are we doing? We are looking for the Dwad in some correct Sign that is equally distant from the nearer Cardinal Point as that Dwad occupied by the Planet (or whatever) we are analyzing.

These two diagrams (Figs. 19 and 20) are taken from my *The Star Wheel Technique,* available from A.F.A.

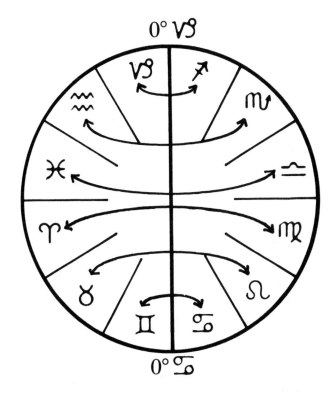

Fig. 19. Diagram for Longitudinal Parallels

The Cardinal Point functions as a midpoint between two equidistant Dwads, subtly linking them together.

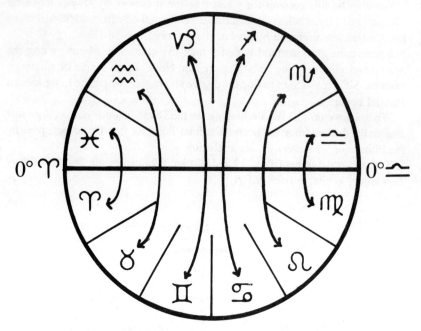

Fig. 20. Diagram for Longitudinal Parallels

Table 29
Cardinal Points Function as a Midpoint
between Two Equidistant Dwads

From 0° Cancer 00′ Solstitial Point	From 0° Aries 00° Equinoctial Point,
Cancer is linked with Gemini	Aries is paired with Pisces
Leo with Taurus	Taurus with Aquarius
Virgo with Aries	Gemini with Capricorn
From 0° Capricorn Solstitial Point	From 0° Libra 00° Equinoctual Point,
Capricorn is linked with Sagittarius	Libra is paired with Virgo
Aquarius with Scorpio	Scorpio with Leo
Pisces with Libra	Sagittarius with Cancer

Just remember to subtract the number of the occupied Dwad from 13 to find the number of the Longitudinal Parallel Dwad in the correct Sign as shown above.

By the way, Miguel Gomez y Peña of Spain suggested the use of ♃ to indicate Longitudinal Parallels.

To Find Natal and Potential Longitudinal Parallels

I first list Natal Planets, etc. in a column. Then I fill in under Aries, Libra and Cancer, Capricorn the required Dwads.

Table 30
To Find Natal and Potential Longitudinal Parallels

Example: Bernard Baruch

Dwads of Natal Placement	Dwads of Longitudinal Parallels from 0° Aries	0° Libra	0° Cancer	0° Capricorn
♆ 9th in ♈	4th in ♓	_____	4th in ♍	_____
♀ 8th in ♉	5th in ♒	_____	5th in ♌	_____
☽ 12th in ♉	1st in ♒	_____	1st in ♌	_____
☽ 1st in ♊	12th in ♑	_____	12th in ♋	_____
♃ 9th in ♊	4th in ♑	_____	4th in ♋	_____
♂ 7th in ♋	_____	6th in ♐	6th in ♊	_____
☊ 8th in ♋	_____	5th in ♐	5th in ♊	_____
♅ 10th in ♋	_____	3rd in ♐	3rd in ♊	_____
♀ 12th in ♋	_____	1st in ♐	1st in ♊	_____
☉ 11th in ♌	_____	2nd in ♏	2nd in ♉	_____
⊗ 7th in ♍	_____	6th in ♎	6th in ♈	_____
☿ 7th in ♍	_____	6th in ♎	6th in ♈	_____
M.C. 11th in ♍	_____	2nd in ♎	2nd in ♈	_____
ASC. 5th in ♐	_____	8th in ♋	_____	8th in ♑
♄ 9th in ♐	_____	4th in ♋	_____	4th in ♑
⊘ 2nd in ♑	11th in ♊	_____	_____	11th in ♐
☋ 8th in ♑	5th in ♊	_____	_____	5th in ♐
⊕ 11th in ♒	2nd in ♉	_____	_____	2nd in ♏

Natal ☊ ⊡ Radix Asc. from 0° ♎
Natal ☋ ⊡ Radix Asc. from 0° ♑
Natal ☽ ⊡ Natal ♀ from 0° ♋

Always take the nearer Equinoctual Point and the nearer Solstitial Point. Longitudinal Parallels, if any, remain powerful factors throughout the entire life. Periods of extra emphasis occur when activated by a Solar Eclipse, etc.

The Cardinal Points are interpreted in their placement in the Natural Zodiacal Wheel, regardless of their placement in the Radix Chart. These four Cardinal Points correspond to the Angles of the Natural Zodiacal Wheel.

The Solstitial Axis relates to heredity and place in life.

The 0° Cancer refers to security generally. Also to estate matters, property, holdings, family, home base, foundation and outcomes generally.

The 0° Capricorn refers to achievement, accomplishment, major projects, career, reputation and standing as well as authority.

The Equinoctial Axis is more personally oriented.

0° Aries — spontaneous activity in personally being or doing.

0° Libra — relatedness, encounters with others, shared interests and activities. A point much affected by others; with, for or against.

Equidistant from 0° Cancer, Mr. Baruch's Natal Moon in Gemini and Venus in Cancer show his natural concern with property, estate matters, foundations and outcomes by connecting an instinct for variables and immediacy (Gemini) linked with fundamental (Cancer) values and attraction.

You can elaborate on this Longitudinal Parallel by combining appropriate Key-words and phrases.

His Natal North Node in Cancer in Longitudinal Parallel Radix Ascendant in Sagittarius measured from 0° Libra, Point of encounters with others, negotiations, dealings, etc., shows his foresighted approach to life (Sagittarius Asc.) which reflects (Longitudinal Parallel) gains, profits, added confidence (North Node) that is fundamental (Cancer).

The Longitudinal Parallel between his South Node — releasing and letting go in timely business matters (Capricorn) that reflect (Parallel) broad yet well aimed approaches (Sagittarius Asc.) measured from 0° Capricorn shows achievement and accomplishment.

When a Natal Planet or other placement occupies a Dwad in Longitudinal Parallel with both Nodes, there may be a flair for letting go.

Liepert stated that each Natal Longitudinal Parallel subtly links the three Dwads involved in a mirroring and reflective way. They link inner and outer, internal and external, psychological and physical in some significant and outstanding way.

What If There is No Longitudinal Parallel at Birth?

Please do not feel deprived if you have none! Many people do not have any at birth.

However, everyone has two *Potential* Longitudinal Parallels to every Planet, True Node, Radix Angle, etc.

The list of Dwads of Natal Planets, etc., with list of Dwads where these Parallels would occur (Table 30) provides a simple way to find when Potential Parallels will be activated by effective Transits, especially by Solar Eclipses and other cycles.

The activation of a Potential Parallel lasts only as long as the focus lasts, for example, a Solar Eclipse would be a focus for approximately three years. Usually you should not allow an Orb beyond the Dwad itself when you note activation of the Potential Parallel by a Solar Eclipse or other effective Transit.

Pairs of Dwad-Hosues

There are six pairs of Dwad-Houses. The sum of their numbers is always 13.

Whenever there is a Natal or Potential Longitudinal Parallel measured from any of the Cardinal Points, one pair of the six pairs is involved.

Table 31
Key-words for Outstanding Feature of Pair (Dwads)

1st	Personal attitudes and own actions, appearances.
& 12th	Intangibles, quiet preparation, covert activities, latent talents.
2nd	Tangibles, assets, talents, profits, support.
& 11th	Circumstances, associates, counseling, important hopes.
3rd	Communication, sequences, local interests, information, mental pursuits.
& 10th	Major projects, authority, reputation, achievement.
4th	Home ground, estate matters, roots, bases, outcome, family.
& 9th	Foreign element, distances, expansion, extension, plan for future.
5th	Heart interests, creativity, showmanship, recreation.
& 8th	Productivity, intense emotion, investigation, joint efforts for mutual benefits, exchange.
6th	Service, skills, technique, craftsmanship, adjustments.
& 7th	Others, public, encounters, fine arts, overt activities, opportunity, reaction.

Most of the Key-words above can be applied to the pair of Dwad-Houses you analyze. The Planets that occupy the Dwad-House and the nature of the Cardinal Point will guide you in your selection of Key-words.

Further Clues for Interpretation of Longitudinal Parallels

After you become fluent in the interpretation of the Dwad-Houses involved, you will likely wish to incorporate the interrelationship of the Dwad-Houses.

The interrelationship between two Dwad-Houses is comparable to the inter-relationship between the two corresponding Houses. For example:

House I is the first of itself	House II is the first of itself
the 2nd of House XII	the 12th of House III
the 3rd of House XI	the 11th of House IV
the 4th of House X, etc.	the 10th of House V, etc.

As we continue all around the Wheel of Houses we find, in a sense, 12 Wheels within each Wheel of Houses.

The House on which we are concentrating, i.e., the House to which we are relating the other Houses, is always the *1st of itself.* That is why, in such,

I say House VII is the 3rd (House) of or from House V. (I think this is clearer than the 7th House in the 3rd House of the 5th House. Of course, the latter is not incorrect; but it can be quite confusing.)

Leipert treated the Wheel of 12 Dwad-Houses very much as earlier astrologers treated the Wheel of Houses, as just given.

If we used a calculated Radix Chart to go around to see the interrelationship between Houses, the sizes of the various Houses probably varied. Nevertheless, regardless of the Tables of Houses used, the entire Wheel of Houses consists of 360°.

Now, our Wheel of Dwad-Houses consists of 30°; so each Dwad-House contains exactly 2½°. Still, the interrelationship between any two Dwad-Houses is the same as between those two corresponding Houses.

Table 32
Interrelationship of the Dwad-Houses of Longitudinal Parallels

(Sum of Dwad-Houses always = 13)

Dwad-House   I =   2nd of Dwad-House XII
Dwad-House   XII =   12th of Dwad-House I
            13   14

Dwad-House   II =   4th of Dwad-House XI
Dwad-House   XI =   10th of Dwad-House II
            13   14

Dwad-House   III =   6th of Dwad-House X
Dwad-House   X =   8th of Dwad-House III
            13   14

Dwad-House   IV =   8th of Dwad-House IX
Dwad-House   IX =   6th of Dwad-House IV
            13   14

Dwad-House   V =   10th of Dwad-House VIII
Dwad-House   VIII =   4th of Dwad-House V
            13   14

Dwad-House   VI =   12th of Dwad-House VII
Dwad-House   VII =   2nd of Dwad-House VI

Example: Bernard Baruch's Natal Moon in Dwad-House I is in Longitudinal Parallel with Natal Venus in Cancer in Dwad-House XII. This Parallel is measured from 0° Cancer.

His personal attitude and own actions are observed and communicated about his feelings and responses to the tenaciously held appreciation and values in the background regarding his roots. He personally has an instinct for hidden or potential values that could be linked with his estate matters and security. Security of 0° Cancer Cardinal Point means "Security" as defined by the individual. For many "Security" includes emotional as well as financial security and personal safety.

This Dwad-House I and XII pair especially, measured from 0° Cancer, tends toward financial activities, the bringing of unknown or unconscious factors to personal action in a supportive way. His attitude toward the intangible factors would note their value and the way he might profit from the generally unknown, etc., etc., etc.

Please reread the above example to note why I chose these Key-words to interpret this Longitudinal Parallel. These are suggestions for you to form your own valid combinations of Key-words.

Use of Dwads in Synastry

In Synastry (Chart Comparison) Leipert relied especially on Conjunctions and Oppositions between the Planets in the Natal Charts involved.

The Conjunctions between Natal Planets show a common ground and a sense of identification with each other. The orb allowed is 10° unless Sun or Moon makes the Conjunction, then he would extend the orb to 12° and up to 14° when the one Sun conjoined the other's Moon.

He allowed the same orb for Oppositions between Natal Planets from one Chart to the other. The Oppositions complement and fulfill, often bringing active cooperation and, sometimes, a challenge. The Oppositions tend toward some kind of relatedness, whether positive or negative. There tends to be some type of encounter with action and reaction involved.

Other Aspects between the Charts he kept to a very narrow orb, as modifiers to the clearly drawn connections shown by the Conjunctions and Oppositions.

Dwad-Signs and Dwad-Houses used in Synastry offer an almost incredible set of clues for a deeper understanding of relationship. What kinds of relationships? Between siblings, between friends, loved ones, between professional colleagues, business associates, employer-employee, professional and clients, parents and children, etc.

To elaborate with specifics and particulars check the placements in the same Dwad-Signs and Dwad-Houses. These show many mutual contacts that would be missed otherwise. All these same Dwad-Signs and Dwad-Houses show a common meeting ground, similarities and a kind of identification.

Then do include placements in opposite Dwad-Signs and Dwad-Houses for complementing characteristics and stimulating contrasts.

Longitudinal Parallels in Synastry

This is an exceptionally important contact between two Natal Charts.

These links between two Natal Charts are easily found and interpreted.

For each analysis I have the Radix and Natal STAR WHEEL, a table of Elements and Qualities, a list of all Natal Aspects, a diagram of Disposition of Planets. In addition to those items I have the Composite Dwad-Wheel and a list of Potential Longitudinal Parallels (see Table 30).

When I compare two Natal Charts I take each list of Potential Longitudinal Parallels. It is easy to see if the other's Natal placements occupy any of the Dwads for Potential Parallels. These are very significant links between the two people.

Any Longitudinal Parallel is very very important. But I give extra significance to the 5th and 8th Dwad-House pair in romantic relationships; this can be an investment of intense emotion. The Leo and Scopio Dwad-Sign combinations can be prominent also.

Other Dwad-House Parallels that give extra emphasis may be the 1st and 12th Dwad-Houses as well as 6th and 7th Dwad-Houses in Longitudinal Parallel.

Libra Dwad-Sign in such a Parallel is very important; so is Aries Dwad-Sign.

Many times in Synastry the Longitudinal Parallels as shown by Dwads tell much of the relationship.

The Use of Dwads in Mundane Astrology

Whether or not you are especially interested in the Mundane branch of Astrology you will, I believe, benefit from this material on the use of Dwads. Of extra importance is the Dwads occupied by the Station — Retrograde or Direct — of some Transiting Planet, a Conjunction between Planets, a New or Full Moon, or Solar or Lunar Eclipse. The Dwads enable us to make a much more comprehensive interpretation of the trends in a world or individual sense.

Along with the Key-words for the Dwad-Houses given in Table 33, you should use those appropriate for the Dwad-Signs. These Dwads give the Focus along with the "specifics and particulars." The meanings of the Signs are even more significant, predominating over the meaning of the Dwads.

Even when no Chart is set up for a definite location on Earth, Eclipses, New and Full Moons, Major Conjunctions, and Stations of Transiting Planets can be interpreted according to the Dwad occupied in the Sign; this is general rather than local, but still highly effective in regard to trends.

When we do not set up a Chart for a Celestial Phenomenon but merely take the degree and minute of the Sign where it occurs directly from the *Ephemeris,* we note the Dwad occupied and interpret accordingly. Use appropriate Key-words for these: Planet or Planets involved, the Dwad-House, the Dwad-Sign, and the Sign itself.

The Dwads are far more specific than are the Decans.

Table 33
A Few Key-words and Phrases for Interests and Activities Shown by Dwads

(Applied to the Dwads in Any Sign)

1st Dwad-House: the general views and efforts of the people.

2nd Dwad-House: values, earning power, assets, possessions.

3rd Dwad-House: transportation, communication, neighbors, boundaries, mental interests, elementary education, news media.

4th Dwad-House: housing, real estate, agriculture, mining, domestic affairs, elderly people, the party "out-of-power" or opposition party.

5th Dwad-House: children, young people, schools, banks, investment, recreation, entertainment, sports, theater, parks, hobbies, romance, birth rate.

6th Dwad-House: health, labor, service (military or civil), employment, tenants, clothing, food (although the 4th relates to crops).

7th Dwad-House: encounters, alliances, cooperation or opposition in the open, negotiations, litigation, dealings with others, public affairs, treaties.

8th Dwad-House: public money, taxes, insurance, money standard, investigation, research, transition, death, retirement.

9th Dwad-House: religion, philosophy, science, law, travel, foreign policy, education, added study, future planning, shipping, publication.

10th Dwad-House: business, government, administration, authority, management, and regulation, status, reputation, achievement, head of state.

11th Dwad-House: circumstances in general, legislation, advisors or counselors, friendly associates, clubs.

12th Dwad-House: "behind the scenes," confidential matters, lodges, secret orders, quiet preparatory activities, espionage, institutions in general, covert activities, exiles, prisoners, hostages, retreats.

Use of Dwads in Horary Astrology

This is not the place to enter into the subject of Horary Astrology and the use of the Dwads. Nevertheless, I feel I must emphasize the great value of the Dwad-Houses and Dwad-Signs in delineating Horary and Electional Charts. The Focuses on pertinent factors are very helpful; the "specifics and particulars" add details.

Why don't you begin by looking up some Horary Charts the outcome of which you already know. Note how the details are indicated by the Dwads occupied.

After you have familiarized yourself with the way the Dwads can be used in this type of Astrology, use the Dwads (in very much the same way you would use them in the analysis of a Natal Chart, as shown in this book) with all Horary and Electional Charts. A whole new dimension is added!

* * * * * * *

You should now have a sound foundation for use of the Dwad Technique in relation to Natal Planets. Furthermore, this material is easily adapted to the analysis of Transits. Use of the Dwads is very helpful when you interpret the trends shown by effective Transits in a personal or worldly sense.

Dwads Occupied by Transits

Leipert found that the Dwad occupied by an Eclipse, New or Full Moon, and effective Transit gives additional clues about what is being activated or highlighted in relation to your own life and world affairs.

(1) Incorporate the Key-words and phrases appropriate to the Dwad when you interpret the Eclipse, New or Full Moon, Planetary Station or other effective Transit. TRUE Nodes may be included. Use Key-words and phrases for Dwad-House and Dwad-Sign.

(2) Look in the Radix Chart to see the Radix House position of the Sign that has the same Name as the Dwad-Sign. This department of life may be activated — without any Transit actually in that House! It is a kind of "echo," a kind of "resonance," so to speak, because of the "tonal correspondence" between the Dwad and the Sign with the same Name.

This is a suggestion as to what can be done to add another dimension — so you can include more than that which is obvious — in your analysis of the meaning of an effective Transit to you personally.

Of course, the Sign in which the Transit occurs is not to be subordinated to the Dwad.

The Sign itself gives the general characterization or description.

The Dwad shows the Focus. It shows the "particulars and specifics."

The Dwad-House helps to specify Who, What, and Where.

The Dwad-Sign helps to detail the description.

The Dwad-Sign also points out the Sign (of the same Name) that acts as a kind of "resonator" and responds to the Transit.

* * * *

Dwads and Transits

Dwads Occupied by Solar Eclipses

Leipert related Solar Eclipses to "history in the making" of the world, nations, states, cities, and of individuals. A Solar Eclipse begins to be effective approximately three months before and continues to be effective for approximately three years after the actual celestial phenomenon occurs. This does not mean that the results do not continue thereafter, but the conscious focus shifts. What has come to the threshold of consciousness remains accessible to consciousness from that time on. Interests and activities begun during that three year period may continue long thereafter.

The Solar Eclipse marks a powerful conscious focus that is truly new or renewed with a new emphasis.

Especially significant personally is a Solar Eclipse that occurs in the same Dwad, or adjacent Dwad, as one occupied by a Natal Planet, House cusp (especially a Radix Angle), True Node, Fortuna or other Arabian Part.

To those who use Longitudinal Parallels from the Equinoctial Points (0° Aries and 0° Libra) and from the Solstitial Points (0° Cancer and 0° Capricorn) I suggest the exact Dwad. The adjacent Dwad seems usually too wide an extension of the orb.

To those who use Midpoints of Planets I suggest the same; use the Dwad that is exact for the Solar Eclipse to focus on the Midpoint.

Wynn used the word "memorable" in relation to Solar Eclipses. They do indeed mark memorable events and periods. Interpretation of the Dwad-House and Dwad-Sign occupied will add considerable detail.

For a Table of Dwads occupied by Solar Eclipses (1900-2000) see Table 34.

Dwads Occupied by Lunar Eclipses

Lunar Eclipses are far less important than Solar Eclipses yet they too should be considered in the Dwad-House and Dwad-Sign occupied.

It begins to be effective approximately 2 or 3 weeks before and continues until about 3 months after the celestial phenomenon. Unless it occurs close to your birthday which is then effective during your entire personal year from birthday to birthday.

Lunar Eclipses tend to fulfill, to settle, to bring about dealings, negotiations, encounters, etc. They nearly always involve others, mate, partner, public, perhaps publicity. Probably there is cooperation, possibly opposition or a challenge of some sort.

I pay some attention to the Dwad occupied by the Sun as well as that occupied by the Eclipsed Moon, in other words, to the pair of opposite Dwads.

There is no list of Lunar Eclipses here, but you can easily compile one for yourself.

Table 34
Dwads of Solar Eclipses 1900-2000

Date	In the Sign	Within the duodenary division	Date	In the Sign	Within the duodenary division
1900 May 28	♊	5°00' to 7°30'	1915 Aug 10	♌	15°00' to 17°30'
1900 Nov 22	♏	27°30' to 30°00'	1916 Feb 3	♒	12°30' to 15°00'
1901 May 18	♉	25°00' to 27°30'	1916 Jul 30	♌	5°00' to 7°30'
1901 Nov 11	♏	17°30' to 20°00'	1916 Dec 24	♑	2°30' to 5°00'
1902 Apr 8	♈	17°30' to 20°00'	1917 Jan 23	♒	2°30' to 5°00'
1902 May 7	♉	15°00' to 17°30'	1917 Jun 19	♊	27°30' to 30°00'
1902 Oct 31	♏	5°00' to 7°30'	1917 Jul 19	♋	25°00' to 27°30'
1903 Mar 29	♈	5°00' to 7°30'	1917 Dec 14	♐	20°00' to 22°30'
1903 Sep 21	♍	25°00' to 27°30'	1918 Jun 8	♊	15°00' to 17°30'
1904 Mar 17	♓	25°00' to 27°30'	1918 Dec 3	♐	10°00' to 12°30'
1904 Sep 9	♍	15°00' to 17°30'	1919 May 29	♊	5°00' to 7°30'
1905 Mar 6	♓	12°30' to 15°00'	1919 Nov 22	♏	27°30' to 30°00'
1905 Aug 30	♍	5°00' to 7°30'	1920 May 18	♉	25°00' to 27°30'
1906 Feb 23	♓	2°30' to 5°00'	1920 Nov 10	♏	17°30' to 20°00'
1906 Jul 21	♋	27°30' to 30°00'	1921 Apr 8	♈	17°30' to 20°00'
1906 Aug 20	♌	25°00' to 27°30'	1921 Oct 1	♎	7°30' to 10°00'
1907 Jan 14	♑	22°30' to 25°00'	1922 Mar 28	♈	5°00' to 7°30'
1907 Jul 10	♋	15°00' to 17°30'	1922 Sep 21	♍	25°00' to 27°30'
1908 Jan 3	♑	10°00' to 12°30'	1923 Mar 17	♓	25°00' to 27°30'
1908 Jun 28	♋	5°00' to 7°30'	1923 Sep 10	♍	15°00' to 17°30'
1908 Dec 23	♑	00°00' to 2°30'	1924 Mar 5	♓	12°30' to 15°00'
1909 Jun 17	♊	25°00' to 27°30'	1924 Jul 31	♌	7°30' to 10°00'
1909 Dec 12	♐	20°00' to 22°30'	1924 Aug 30	♍	5°00' to 7°30'
1910 May 9	♉	17°30' to 20°00'	1925 Jan 24	♒	2°30' to 5°00'
1910 Nov 12	♏	7°30' to 10°00'	1925 Jul 20	♋	27°30' to 30°00'
1911 Apr 28	♉	7°30' to 10°00'	1926 Jan 14	♑	22°30' to 25°00'
1911 Oct 22	♎	27°30' to 30°00'	1926 Jul 9	♋	15°00' to 17°30'
1912 Apr 17	♈	25°00' to 27°30'	1927 Jan 3	♑	10°00' to 12°30'
1912 Oct 10	♎	15°00' to 17°30'	1927 Jun 29	♋	5°00' to 7°30'
1913 Apr 6	♈	15°00' to 17°30'	1927 Dec 24	♑	00°00' to 2°30'
1913 Aug 31	♍	7°30' to 10°00'	1928 May 19	♉	27°30' to 30°00'
1913 Sep 30	♎	5°00' to 7°30'	1928 Jun 17	♊	25°00' to 27°30'
1914 Feb 25	♓	5°00' to 7°30'	1928 Nov 12	♏	17°30' to 20°00'
1914 Aug 21	♌	27°30' to 30°00'	1929 May 9	♉	17°30' to 20°00'
1915 Feb 14	♒	22°30' to 25°00'	1929 Nov 1	♏	7°30' to 10°00'

Table 34 (continued)

1930 Apr 28	♉	7°30' to 10°00'	1946 Nov 23	♐	00°00' to 2°30'
1930 Oct 21	♎	27°30' to 30°00'	1947 May 20	♉	27°30' to 30°00'
1931 Apr 18	♈	25°00' to 27°30'	1947 Nov 12	♏	17°30' to 20°00'
1931 Sep 12	♍	17°30' to 20°00'	1948 May 9	♉	17°30' to 20°00'
1931 Oct 11	♎	15°00' to 17°30'	1948 Nov 1	♏	7°30' to 10°00'
1932 Mar 7	♓	15°00' to 17°30'	1949 Apr 28	♉	7°30' to 10°00'
1932 Aug 31	♍	7°30' to 10°00'	1949 Oct 21	♎	27°30' to 30°00'
1933 Feb 24	♓	5°00' to 7°30'	1950 Mar 18	♓	25°00' to 27°30'
1933 Aug 21	♌	27°30' to 30°00'	1950 Sep 12	♍	17°30' to 20°00'
1934 Feb 14	♒	22°30' to 25°00'	1951 Mar 7	♓	15°00' to 17°30'
1934 Aug 10	♌	15°00' to 17°30'	1951 Sep 1	♍	7°30' to 10°00'
1935 Jan 5	♑	12°30' to 15°00'	1952 Feb 25	♓	5°00' to 7°30'
1935 Feb 3	♒	12°30' to 15°00'	1952 Aug 20	♌	27°30' to 30°00'
1935 Jun 30	♋	7°30' to 10°00'	1953 Feb 14	♒	25°00' to 27°30'
1935 Jul 30	♌	5°00' to 7°30'	1953 Jul 11	♋	17°30' to 20°00'
1935 Dec 25	♑	2°30' to 5°00'	1953 Aug 9	♌	15°00' to 17°30'
1936 Jun 19	♊	27°30' to 30°00'	1954 Jan 5	♑	12°30' to 15°00'
1936 Dec 13	♐	20°00' to 22°30'	1954 Jun 30	♋	7°30' to 10°00'
1937 Jun 8	♊	17°30' to 20°00'	1954 Dec 25	♑	2°30' to 5°00'
1937 Dec 2	♐	10°00' to 12°30'	1955 Jun 20	♊	27°30' to 30°00'
1938 May 29	♊	7°30' to 10°00'	1955 Dec 14	♐	20°00' to 22°30'
1938 Nov 22	♏	27°30' to 30°00'	1956 Jun 8	♊	17°30' to 20°00'
1939 Apr 19	♈	27°30' to 30°00'	1956 Dec 2	♐	10°00' to 12°30'
1939 Oct 12	♎	17°30' to 20°00'	1957 Apr 29	♉	7°30' to 10°00'
1940 Apr 7	♈	17°30' to 20°00'	1957 Oct 23	♎	27°30' to 30°00'
1940 Oct 1	♎	7°30' to 10°00'	1958 Apr 19	♈	27°30' to 30°00'
1941 Mar 27	♈	5°00' to 7°30'	1958 Oct 12	♎	17°30' to 20°00'
1941 Sep 21	♍	27°30' to 30°00'	1959 Apr 8	♈	17°30' to 20°00'
1942 Mar 16	♓	25°00' to 27°30'	1959 Oct 2	♎	7°30' to 10°00'
1942 Aug 12	♌	17°30' to 20°00'	1960 Mar 27	♈	5°00' to 7°30'
1942 Sep 10	♍	15°00' to 17°30'	1960 Sep 20	♍	27°30' to 30°00'
1943 Feb 4	♒	15°00' to 17°30'	1961 Feb 15	♒	25°00' to 27°30'
1943 Aug 1	♌	7°30' to 10°00'	1961 Aug 11	♌	17°30' to 20°00'
1944 Jan 25	♒	2°30' to 5°00'	1962 Feb 5	♒	15°00' to 17°30'
1944 Jul 20	♋	25°00' to 27°30'	1962 Jul 31	♌	7°30' to 10°00'
1945 Jan 14	♑	22°30' to 25°00'	1963 Jan 25	♒	2°30' to 5°00'
1945 Jul 9	♋	15°00' to 17°30'	1963 Jul 20	♋	25°00' to 27°30'
1946 Jan 3	♑	12°30' to 15°00'	1964 Jan 14	♑	22°30' to 25°00'
1946 May 30	♊	7°30' to 10°00'	1964 Jun 10	♊	17°30' to 20°00'
1946 Jun 29	♋	5°00' to 7°30'	1964 Jul 9	♋	15°00' to 17°30'

Table 34 (continued)

Date	Sign	Range	Date	Sign	Range
1964 Dec 4	♐	10°00' to 12°30'	1982 Dec 15	♐	22°30' to 25°00'
1965 May 30	♊	7°30' to 10°00'	1983 Jun 11	♊	17°30' to 20°00'
1965 Nov 23	♐	00°00' to 2°30'	1983 Dec 4	♐	10°00' to 12°30'
1966 May 20	♉	27°30' to 30°00'	1984 May 20	♊	7°30' to 10°00'
1966 Nov 12	♏	17°30' to 20°00'	1984 Nov 22	♐	00°00' to 2°30'
1967 May 9	♉	17°30' to 20°00'	1985 May 19	♉	27°30' to 30°00'
1967 Nov 2	♏	7°30' to 10°00'	1985 Nov 12	♏	20°00' to 22°30'
1968 Mar 28	♈	7°30' to 10°00'	1986 Apr 9	♈	17°30' to 20°00'
1968 Sep 22	♍	27°30' to 30°00'	1986 Oct 3	♎	10°00' to 12°30'
1969 Mar 18	♓	25°00' to 27°30'	1987 Mar 29	♈	7°30' to 10°00'
1969 Sep 11	♍	17°30' to 20°00'	1987 Sep 23	♍	27°30' to 30°00'
1970 Mar 7	♓	15°00' to 17°30'	1988 Mar 18	♓	27°30' to 30°00'
1970 Aug 31	♍	7°30' to 10°00'	1988 Sep 11	♍	17°30' to 20°00'
1971 Feb 25	♓	5°00' to 7°30'	1989 Mar 7	♓	15°00' to 17°30'
1971 Jul 22	♋	27°30' to 30°00'	1989 Aug 31	♍	7°30' to 10°00'
1971 Aug 20	♌	25°00' to 27°30'	1990 Jan 26	♒	5°00' to 7°30'
1972 Jan 16	♑	25°00' to 27°30'	1990 Jul 22	♋	27°30' to 30°00'
1972 Jul 10	♋	17°30' to 20°00'	1991 Jan 15	♑	25°00' to 27°30'
1973 Jan 4	♑	12°30' to 15°00'	1991 July 11	♋	17°30' to 20°00'
1973 Jun 30	♋	7°30' to 10°00'	1992 Jan 4	♑	12°30' to 15°00'
1973 Dec 24	♑	2°30' to 5°00'	1992 Jun 30	♋	7°30' to 10°00'
1974 Jun 20	♊	27°30' to 30°00'	1992 Dec 24	♑	00°00' to 2°30'
1974 Dec 13	♐	20°00' to 22°30'	1993 May 21	♊	00°00' to 2°30'
1975 May 11	♉	17°30' to 20°00'	1993 Nov 13	♏	20°00' to 22°30'
1975 Nov 3	♏	10°00' to 12°30'	1994 May 10	♉	17°30' to 20°00'
1976 Apr 29	♉	7°30' to 10°00'	1994 Nov 3	♏	10°00' to 12°30'
1976 Oct 23	♎	27°30' to 30°00'	1995 Apr 29	♉	7°30' to 10°00'
1977 Apr 18	♈	27°30' to 30°00'	1995 Oct 24	♏	00°00' to 2°30'
1977 Oct 12	♎	17°30' to 20°00'	1996 Apr 17	♈	27°30' to 30°00'
1978 Apr 7	♈	15°00' to 17°30'	1996 Oct 12	♎	17°30' to 20°00'
1978 Oct 2	♎	7°30' to 10°00'	1997 Mar 9	♓	17°30' to 20°00'
1979 Feb 26	♓	5°00' to 7°30'	1997 Sep 2	♍	7°30' to 10°00'
1979 Aug 22	♌	27°30' to 30°00'	1998 Feb 26	♓	7°30' to 10°00'
1980 Feb 16	♒	25°00' to 27°30'	1998 Aug 22	♌	27°30' to 30°00'
1980 Aug 10	♌	17°30' to 20°00'	1999 Feb 16	♒	25°00' to 27°30'
1981 Feb 4	♒	15°00' to 17°30'	1999 Aug 11	♌	17°30' to 20°00'
1981 Jul 31	♌	7°30' to 10°00'	2000 Feb 5	♒	15°00' to 17°30'
1982 Jan 25	♒	2°30' to 5°00'	2000 Jul 1	♋	10°00' to 12°30'
1982 Jun 21	♊	27°30' to 30°00'	2000 Jul 31	♌	7°30' to 10°00'
1982 Jul 20	♋	27°30' to 30°00'	2000 Dec 25	♑	2°30' to 5°00'

Dwads Occupied by New and Full Moons

Not only are Lunations very important in Mundane Astrology, they should be noted as activators of Natal Charts, especially when either occurs in the same Dwad occupied by the Natal Lights, Planets, House Cusps (especially Radix Angles), True Nodes, Fortuna, or other Sensitive Points.

The Lunation very close to the birthday marks a "New Moon Year" or a "Full Moon Year." Otherwise, the New Moon is effective for four weeks and the Full Moon for two weeks.

Remember to interpret the Dwad occupied in relation to world trends in Mundane Astrology as well as personal trends in Natal Astrology.

There is no list of New or Full Moons here, but you may easily make one yourself. The current ephemeris will give the New and Full Moons.

Transits in the Natal Sun-Sign
or in the Sign of the Transiting Sun

Leipert noted that all New and Full Moons and especially Eclipses are more or less important in relation to the Chart of an individual.

However, he found that some Stations of Transiting Planets and some Major Conjunctions are of great personal significance while others are not. In any case, whether of personal significance or not, they do show what is going on around the individual. This is a very important observation.

Any Transit in your Sun-Sign is more or less important to you. Leipert stated it this way: "Your Natal Sun-Sign may be likened to a Gate of Consciousness; this 'Gate' remains 'open' throughout your entire lifetime. So every Transit through your Sun-Sign is an effective Transit with a directly individual significance."

He added that Transits in the same Sign as the Transiting Sun are also effective for everyone, more or less. The interpretation varies according to the individual Charts and the level on which the person is living.

The slower moving Planets (Mars, Jupiter, Saturn, etc.) do not ever have their Stations in the Sign of the Transiting Sun; they may occur in your Natal Sun Sign.

It is not customary for even the faster moving Mercury and Venus to have their Stations in the Sign of the Transiting Sun; they occur more frequently in the adjacent Sign.

When Mercury has its Station in the Sign of the Transiting Sun, it should be noted in relation to individual and mundane Charts. What is indicated may not be of tremendous importance but it usually calls our attention.

Dwads Occupied by Planetary Stations

The following list is for 1984 when there are many Retrograde Planets at about the same time. It is dated material. Nevertheless, it is a good example for you to follow when you make your own for any other year.

Table 35
List of Retrograde and Direct Stations

	Planet		Sign	Dwad	Dwad-House	Dwad-Sign
1983						
Dec 22	☿	SR in	16 ♑ 38	7th	7th	♋
1984						
Jan 11	☿	SD in	0 ♑ 23	1st	1st	♑
Feb 4	♇	SR in	2 ♏ 08	1st	1st	♏
Feb 24	♄	SR in	16 ♏ 23	7th	7th	♉
Mar 18	♅	SR	13 ♐ 34	6th	6th	♉
Apr 2	♆	SR	1 ♑ 26	1st	1st	♑
Apr 5	♂	SR	28 ♏ 21	12th	12th	♎
Apr 11	☿	SR	6 ♉ 40	3rd	3rd	♋
Apr 29	♃	SR	12 ♑ 58	6th	6th	♊
May 5	☿	SD	26 ♈ 19	11th	11th	♒
Jun 19	♂	SD	11 ♏ 42	5th	5th	♓
Jul 9	♇	SD	29 ♎ 19	12th	12th	♍
Jul 13	♄	SD	9 ♏ 42	4th	4th	♒
Aug 14	☿	SR	13 ♍ 22	6th	6th	♒
Aug 18	♅	SD	9 ♐ 32	4th	4th	♓
Aug 29	♃	SD	3 ♑ 08	2nd	2nd	♒
Sep 7	☿	SD	0 ♍ 02	1st	1st	♍
Sep 9	♆	SD	28 ♐ 39	12th	12th	♏
Dec 4	☿	SR	0 ♑ 44	1st	1st	♑
Dec 24	☿	SD	14 ♐ 33	6th	6th	♉
1985						
Mar 13	♀	SR	22 ♈ 17	9th	9th	♐
Apr 25	♀	SD	6 ♈ 00	3rd	3rd	♊

Mercury Retrograde (Transiting)

Each time Transiting Mercury apparently goes Retrograde, there tends to be a reviewing of some kind, introspection, retrospection, etc. It is an excellent time for editing, rereading something important, rechecking calculations, etc. It often is favorable for getting in touch with lapsed contacts, perhaps for paying or collecting accounts that are in arrears. This is, of course, a general interpretation of the trend when Mercury is retrograde; it is generally applicable whenever Mercury is Retrograde. But these Retrograde periods of Transiting Mercury may not be equally significant to you individually.

However, when the Retrograde Station is in your Natal Sun-Sign or in a Dwad-Sign which corresponds to your Natal Sun-Sign or in the Sign occupied by the Sun at the time of the Station (as listed above), there may be some personal significance for you.

Mercury Stationary Direct

When this occurs in your own Natal Sun-Sign, or even in a Dwad-Sign with the same Name as your Sun-Sign, or in the Sign occupied by the Transiting Sun, it may mark something individually meaningful to you: information, concepts, ideas, etc., which may involve messages, books, news, communications, etc. Note the Dwad for more specifics.

Dwads Occupied by Major Conjunctions

Each Major Conjunction is a sensitive point until the same two Planets make their next Conjunction.

Not all of these Major Conjunctions have personal significance but they show what is going on in the world. Perhaps they have a direct personal impact as well, very much so when the Conjunction occurs in the Natal Sun-Sign.

One Major Conjunction Leipert always placed alongside the Natal Chart: the Jupiter-Saturn Conjunction prior to birth. Be sure to take the one prior to birth even though it occurred nearly 20 years before birth. Leipert affirmed that it remained a Sensitive Point all through life. It indicates your particular "niche" in life, where and how you belong, the structure or framework or lifestyle (Saturn) in which you can function most freely and beneficially (Jupiter). So, by considering the Dwad-House and Dwad-Sign occupied you have specifics and particulars to add to the meanings of Sign and House occupied.

Conjunctions

Mars conjunct Jupiter, Saturn, Uranus, Neptune, Pluto, occurs about every two years.

Jupiter conjunct Saturn occurs about every 20 years.
Jupiter conjunct Uranus occurs about every 14 years.
Jupiter conjunct Neptune occurs about every 13 years.
Jupiter conjunct Pluto occurs about every 12 years.
Saturn conjunct Uranus occurs about every 45 years.
Saturn conjunct Neptune occurs about every 36 years.
Saturn conjunct Pluto occurs about every 33 years.
Uranus conjunct Neptune occurs about every 171 years.
Uranus conjunct Pluto occurs about every 127 years.
Neptune conjunct Pluto occurs about every 490 years.

Table 36
Dwads of Major Conjunctions 1900-2000

Date	In the Sign	Within the duodenary division	Date	In the Sign	Within the duodenary division
MARS CONJUNCTION JUPITER					
1899 Oct 11	♏	12°30' to 15°00'	1953 Apr 27	♉	25°00' to 27°30'
1901 Dec 17	♑	17°30' to 20°00'	1955 Jul 25	♌	7°30' to 10°00'
1904 Feb 25	♓	27°30' to 30°00'	1957 Oct 16	♎	12°30' to 15°00'
1906 May 18	♊	12°30' to 15°00'	1959 Dec 28	♐	17°30' to 20°00'
1908 Aug 14	♌	22°30' to 25°00'	1962 Mar 6	♒	25°00' to 27°30'
1910 Nov 4	♎	27°30' to 30°00'	1964 May 19	♉	7°30' to 10°00'
1913 Jan 13	♑	2°30' to 5°00'	1966 Aug 12	♋	20°00' to 22°30'
1915 Mar 24	♓	10°00' to 12°30'	1968 Nov 6	♍	27°30' to 30°00'
1917 Jun 8	♉	25°00' to 27°30'	1971 Jan 26	♐	00°00' to 2°30'
1919 Sep 2	♌	5°00' to 7°30'	1973 Apr 6	♒	7°30' to 10°00'
1921 Nov 27	♎	10°00' to 12°30'	1975 Jun 16	♈	17°30' to 20°00'
1924 Feb 13	♐	15°00' to 17°30'	1977 Sep 4	♋	00°00' to 2°30'
1926 Apr 23	♒	22°30' to 25°00'	1979 Dec 15	♍	10°00' to 12°30'
1928 Jul 4	♉	5°00' to 7°30'	1980 Feb 27	♍	2°30' to 5°00'
1930 Sep 27	♋	17°30' to 20°00'	1980 May 5	♍	00°00' to 2°30'
1933 Jun 4	♍	12°30' to 15°00'	1982 Aug 8	♏	2°30' to 5°00'
1935 Aug 26	♏	15°00' to 17°30'	1984 Oct 14	♑	5°00' to 7°30'
1937 Oct 30	♑	20°00' to 22°30'	1986 Dec 18	♓	15°00' to 17°30'
1940 Jan 6	♈	00°00' to 2°30'	1989 Mar 11	♊	00°00' to 2°30'
1942 Apr 3	♊	15°00' to 17°30'	1991 Jun 13	♌	10°00' to 12°30'
1944 Jul 5	♌	25°00' to 27°30'	1993 Sep 6	♎	15°00' to 17°30'
1946 Sep 24	♎	27°30' to 30°00'	1995 Nov 16	♐	17°30' to 20°00'
1948 Dec 1	♑	2°30' to 5°00'	1998 Jan 21	♒	25°00' to 27°30'
1951 Feb 7	♓	12°30' to 15°00'	2000 Apr 6	♉	10°00' to 12°30'
MARS CONJUNCT SATURN					
1899 Dec 6	♐	22°30' to 25°00'	1919 Oct 24	♍	7°30' to 10°00'
1901 Dec 14	♑	15°00' to 17°30'	1921 Nov 13	♎	2°30' to 5°00'
1903 Dec 21	♒	5°00' to 7°30'	1923 Dec 1	♎	27°30' to 30°00'
1905 Dec 25	♒	27°30' to 30°00'	1925 Dec 14	♏	20°00' to 22°30'
1907 Dec 30	♓	20°00' to 22°30'	1927 Dec 26	♐	12°30' to 15°00'
1909 Dec 29	♈	15°00' to 17°30'	1930 Jan 3	♑	2°30' to 5°00'
1911 Aug 16	♉	17°30' to 20°00'	1932 Jan 11	♑	25°00' to 27°30'
1913 Aug 24	♊	15°00' to 17°30'	1934 Jan 17	♒	15°00' to 17°30'
1915 Sep 11	♋	12°30' to 15°00'	1936 Jan 25	♓	7°30' to 10°00'
1917 Oct 1	♌	10°00' to 12°30'	1938 Feb 1	♈	00°00' to 2°30'

87

Table 36 (continued)

1940 Feb 11	♈	25°00' to 27°30'		1970 Mar 15	♉	5°00' to 7°30'
1942 Feb 22	♉	20°00' to 22°30'		1972 Mar 31	♊	2°30' to 5°00'
1944 Mar 7	♊	17°30' to 20°00'		1974 Apr 20	♋	00°00' to 2°30'
1945 Oct 26	♋	22°30' to 25°00'		1976 May 12	♋	27°30' to 30°00'
1946 Jan 20	♋	20°00' to 22°30'		1978 Jun 3	♌	25°00' to 27°30'
1946 Mar 20	♋	17°30' to 20°00'		1980 Jun 24	♍	20°00' to 22°30'
1947 Nov 12	♌	20°00' to 22°30'		1982 Jul 7	♎	15°00' to 17°30'
1949 Nov 30	♍	17°30' to 20°00'		1984 Feb 15	♏	15°00' to 17°30'
1951 Dec 18	♎	12°30' to 15°00'		1986 Feb 17	♐	7°30' to 10°00'
1954 Jan 2	♏	7°30' to 10°00'		1988 Feb 23	♑	00°00' to 2°30'
1956 Jan 14	♐	00°00' to 2°30'		1990 Feb 28	♑	20°00' to 22°30'
1958 Jan 23	♐	20°00' to 22°30'		1992 Mar 6	♒	12°30' to 15°00'
1960 Jan 31	♑	12°30' to 15°00'		1994 Mar 14	♓	5°00' to 7°30'
1962 Feb 7	♒	2°30' to 5°00'		1996 Mar 22	♓	27°30' to 30°00'
1964 Feb 14	♒	25°00' to 27°30'		1998 Apr 2	♈	20°00' to 22°30'
1966 Feb 21	♓	17°30' to 20°00'		2000 Apr 15	♉	15°00' to 17°30'
1968 Mar 2	♈	10°00' to 12°30'				

MARS CONJUNCT URANUS

1899 Nov 13	♐	5°00' to 7°30'		1938 Mar 28	♉	10°00' to 12°30'
1901 Nov 4	♐	15°00' to 17°30'		1940 Mar 16	♉	17°30' to 20°00'
1903 Oct 24	♐	22°30' to 25°00'		1942 Mar 1	♉	25°00' to 27°30'
1905 Oct 8	♑	00°00' to 2°30'		1943 Sep 9	♊	7°30' to 10°00'
1907 May 2	♑	12°30' to 15°00'		1943 Dec 30	♊	5°00' to 7°30'
1909 Mar 26	♑	20°00' to 22°30'		1944 Jan 16	♊	5°00' to 7°30'
1911 Mar 11	♑	27°30' to 30°00'		1945 Aug 17	♊	15°00' to 17°30'
1913 Feb 26	♒	5°00' to 7°30'		1947 Aug 6	♊	22°30' to 25°00'
1915 Feb 15	♒	10°00' to 12°30'		1949 Jul 27	♋	2°30' to 5°00'
1917 Feb 3	♒	17°30' to 20°00'		1951 Jul 20	♋	10°00' to 12°30'
1919 Jan 22	♒	25°00' to 27°30'		1953 Jul 12	♋	17°30' to 20°00'
1921 Jan 9	♓	2°30' to 5°00'		1955 Jul 6	♋	25°00' to 27°30'
1922 Dec 25	♓	10°00' to 12°30'		1957 Jun 29	♌	5°00' to 7°30'
1924 Nov 27	♓	17°30' to 20°00'		1959 Jun 24	♌	12°30' to 15°00'
1926 Jun 13	♓	27°30' to 30°00'		1961 Jun 16	♌	22°30' to 25°00'
1928 May 25	♈	5°00' to 7°30'		1963 Jun 6	♍	00°00' to 2°30'
1930 May 12	♈	12°30' to 15°00'		1964 Dec 6	♍	12°30' to 15°00'
1932 Apr 29	♈	20°00' to 22°30'		1966 Nov 22	♍	22°30' to 25°00'
1934 Apr 19	♈	25°00' to 27°30'		1968 Nov 13	♎	2°30' to 5°00'
1936 Apr 7	♉	2°30' to 5°00'		1970 Nov 7	♎	10°00' to 12°30'

Table 36 (continued)

1972 Oct 31	♎	17°30' to 20°00'	1988 Feb 21	♑	00°00' to 2°30'
1974 Oct 26	♎	27°30' to 30°00'	1990 Feb 9	♑	7°30' to 10°00'
1976 Oct 18	♏	5°00' to 7°30'	1992 Jan 29	♑	15°00' to 17°30'
1978 Oct 11	♏	12°30' to 15°00'	1994 Jan 18	♑	22°30' to 25°00'
1980 Oct 2	♏	22°30' to 25°00'	1996 Jan 8	♑	27°30' to 30°00'
1982 Sep 20	♐	00°00' to 2°30'	1997 Dec 27	♒	5°00' to 7°30'
1984 Sep 3	♐	7°30' to 10°00'	1999 Dec 14	♒	12°30' to 15°00'
1986 Mar 13	♐	20°00' to 22°30'			

MARS CONJUNCT NEPTUNE

1900 Aug 7	♊	27°30' to 30°00'	1952 Jan 2	♎	20°00' to 22°30'
1902 Jul 24	♋	00°00' to 2°30'	1953 Dec 13	♎	25°00' to 27°30'
1904 Jul 9	♋	5°00' to 7°30'	1955 Nov 27	♎	27°30' to 30°00'
1906 Jun 26	♋	7°30' to 10°00'	1957 Nov 13	♏	2°30' to 5°00'
1908 Jun 12	♋	12°30' to 15°00'	1959 Oct 31	♏	5°00' to 7°30'
1910 May 30	♋	17°30' to 20°00'	1961 Oct 17	♏	10°00' to 12°30'
1912 May 13	♋	20°00' to 22°30'	1963 Oct 3	♏	12°30' to 15°00'
1914 Apr 22	♋	25°00' to 27°30'	1965 Sep 16	♏	17°30' to 20°00'
1915 Oct 12	♌	2°30' to 5°00'	1967 Aug 28	♏	20°00' to 22°30'
1917 Sep 22	♌	5°00' to 7°30'	1969 Feb 22	♏	27°30' to 30°00'
1919 Sep 8	♌	10°00' to 12°30'	1971 Jan 27	♐	2°30' to 5°00'
1921 Aug 25	♌	12°30' to 15°00'	1973 Jan 9	♐	5°00' to 7°30'
1923 Aug 13	♌	17°30' to 20°00'	1974 Dec 25	♐	10°00' to 12°30'
1925 Jul 30	♌	20°00' to 22°30'	1976 Dec 10	♐	12°30' to 15°00'
1927 Jul 18	♌	25°00' to 27°30'	1978 Nov 26	♐	17°30' to 20°00'
1929 Jul 3	♌	27°30' to 30°00'	1980 Nov 10	♐	20°00' to 22°30'
1931 Jun 16	♍	2°30' to 5°00'	1982 Oct 25	♐	22°30' to 25°00'
1933 May 17	♍	5°00' to 7°30'	1984 Oct 3	♐	27°30' to 30°00'
1934 Nov 11	♍	12°30' to 15°00'	1986 Apr 9	♑	5°00' to 7°30'
1936 Oct 25	♍	17°30' to 20°00'	1988 Mar 8	♑	7°30' to 10°00'
1938 Oct 12	♍	20°00' to 22°30'	1990 Feb 17	♑	12°30' to 15°00'
1940 Sep 28	♍	25°00' to 27°30'	1992 Feb 1	♑	15°00' to 17°30'
1942 Sep 16	♍	27°30' to 30°00'	1994 Jan 16	♑	20°00' to 22°30'
1944 Sep 2	♎	2°30' to 5°00'	1996 Jan 1	♑	22°30' to 25°00'
1946 Aug 20	♎	5°00' to 7°30'	1997 Dec 16	♑	27°30' to 30°00'
1948 Aug 4	♎	10°00' to 12°30'	1999 Nov 29	♒	00°00' to 2°30'
1950 Jul 14	♎	12°30' to 15°00'			

Table 36 (continued)

MARS CONJUNCT PLUTO

Date	Sign	Range	Date	Sign	Range
1900 Jul 21	♊	15°00' to 17°30'	1951 Sep 19	♌	20°00' to 22°30'
1902 Jul 4	♊	17°30' to 20°00'	1953 Sep 4	♌	22°30' to 25°00'
1904 Jun 16	♊	20°00' to 22°30'	1955 Aug 21	♌	25°00' to 27°30'
1906 May 30	♊	20°00' to 22°30'	1957 Aug 7	♌	27°30' to 30°00'
1908 May 12	♊	22°30' to 25°00'	1959 Jul 25	♍	2°30' to 5°00'
1910 Apr 24	♊	25°00' to 27°30'	1961 Jul 9	♍	5°00' to 7°30'
1912 Mar 30	♊	25°00' to 27°30'	1963 Jun 22	♍	7°30' to 10°00'
1913 Sep 17	♋	00°00' to 2°30'	1964 Dec 10	♍	15°00' to 17°30'
1915 Aug 24	♋	2°30' to 5°00'	1966 Nov 16	♍	20°00' to 22°30'
1917 Aug 4	♋	2°30' to 5°00'	1968 Oct 30	♍	22°30' to 25°00'
1919 Jul 18	♋	5°00' to 7°30'	1970 Oct 17	♍	27°30' to 30°00'
1921 Jul 1	♋	7°30' to 10°00'	1972 Oct 4	♎	00°00' to 2°30'
1923 Jun 15	♋	10°00' to 12°30'	1974 Sep 22	♎	5°00' to 7°30'
1925 May 29	♋	10°00' to 12°30'	1976 Sep 9	♎	10°00' to 12°30'
1927 May 11	♋	12°30' to 15°00'	1978 Aug 28	♎	15°00' to 17°30'
1929 Apr 16	♋	15°00' to 17°30'	1980 Aug 12	♎	17°30' to 20°00'
1930 Oct 2	♋	20°00' to 22°30'	1982 Jul 24	♎	22°30' to 25°00'
1932 Sep 9	♋	22°30' to 25°00'	1984 Jan 15	♏	00°00' to 2°30'
1934 Aug 23	♋	25°00' to 27°30'	1985 Dec 25	♏	5°00' to 7°30'
1936 Aug 6	♋	25°00' to 27°30'	1987 Dec 11	♏	10°00' to 12°30'
1938 Jul 22	♋	27°30' to 30°00'	1989 Nov 27	♏	15°00' to 17°30'
1940 Jul 6	♌	00°00' to 2°30'	1991 Nov 15	♏	20°00' to 22°30'
1942 Jun 21	♌	2°30' to 5°00'	1993 Nov 1	♏	22°30' to 25°00'
1944 Jun 3	♌	5°00' to 7°30'	1995 Oct 19	♏	27°30' to 30°00'
1946 May 13	♌	7°30' to 10°00'	1997 Oct 4	♐	2°30' to 5°00'
1947 Oct 28	♌	12°30' to 15°00'	1999 Sep 15	♐	7°30' to 10°00'
1949 Oct 6	♌	17°30' to 20°00'			

JUPITER CONJUNCT SATURN

Date	Sign	Range	Date	Sign	Range
1901 Nov 28	♑	12°30' to 15°00'	1961 Feb 19	♑	25°00' to 27°30'
1921 Sep 10	♍	25°00' to 27°30'	1980 Dec 31	♎	7°30' to 10°00'
1940 Aug 8	♉	12°30' to 15°00'	1981 Mar 3	♎	7°30' to 10°00'
1940 Oct 20	♉	10°00' to 12°30'	1981 Jul 24	♎	2°30' to 5°00'
1941 Feb 15	♉	7°30' to 10°00'	2000 May 28	♉	22°30' to 25°00'

JUPITER CONJUNCT URANUS

Date	Sign	Range	Date	Sign	Range
1900 Oct 20	♐	10°00' to 12°30'	1941 May 8	♉	25°00' to 27°30'
1914 Mar 4	♒	7°30' to 10°00'	1954 Oct 7	♋	25°00' to 27°30'
1927 Jul 15	♈	2°30' to 5°00'	1955 Jan 7	♋	25°00' to 27°30'
1927 Aug 11	♈	2°30' to 5°00'	1955 May 10	♋	22°30' to 25°00'
1928 Jan 25	♈	00°00' to 2°30'	1968 Dec 11	♎	2°30' to 5°00'

Table 36 (continued)

1969 Mar 11	♎	00°00' to 2°30'	1983 May 15	♐	7°30' to 10°00'
1969 Jul 20	♎	00°00' to 2°30'	1983 Sep 25	♐	5°00' to 7°30'
1983 Feb 18	♐	7°30' to 10°00'	1997 Feb 16	♒	5°00' to 7°30'

JUPITER CONJUNCT NEPTUNE

1907 May 22	♋	10°00' to 12°30'	1958 Sep 24	♏	2°30' to 5°00'
1919 Sep 24	♌	10°00' to 12°30'	1971 Feb 1	♐	2°30' to 5°00'
1920 Mar 8	♌	7°30' to 10°00'	1971 May 22	♐	00°00' to 2°30'
1920 Apr 24	♌	7°30' to 10°00'	1971 Sep 16	♐	00°00' to 2°30'
1932 Sep 19	♍	7°30' to 10°00'	1984 Jan 19	♑	00°00' to 2°30'
1945 Sep 22	♎	5°00' to 7°30'	1997 Jan 9	♑	25°00' to 27°30'

JUPITER CONJUNCT PLUTO

1906 Jun 26	♊	22°30' to 25°00'	1956 Feb 8	♌	27°30' to 30°00'
1918 Aug 10	♋	5°00' to 7°30'	1956 Jun 16	♌	25°00' to 27°30'
1931 May 27	♋	17°30' to 20°00'	1968 Oct 13	♍	22°30' to 25°00'
1943 Aug 1	♌	5°00' to 7°30'	1981 Nov 2	♎	22°30' to 25°00'
1955 Nov 2	♌	27°30' to 30°00'	1994 Dec 2	♏	27°30' to 30°00'

SATURN CONJUNCT URANUS

1897 Sep 9	♏	25°00' to 27°30'	1988 Jun 26	♐	27°30' to 30°00'
1942 May 3	♉	27°30' to 30°00'	1988 Sep 18	♐	27°30' to 30°00'
1988 Feb 13	♑	27°30' to 30°00'			

SATURN CONJUNCT NEPTUNE

1917 Aug 1	♌	2°30' to 5°00'	1989 Mar 3	♑	10°00' to 12°30'
1952 Nov 21	♎	22°30' to 25°00'	1989 Jun 24	♑	10°00' to 12°30'
1953 May 17	♎	20°00' to 22°30'	1989 Nov 13	♑	10°00' to 12°30'
1953 Jul 22	♎	20°00' to 22°30'			

SATURN CONJUNCT PLUTO

1914 Oct 4	♋	00°00' to 2°30'	1947 Aug 11	♌	12°30' to 15°00'
1914 Nov 1	♋	00°00' to 2°30'	1982 Nov 8	♎	27°30' to 30°00'
1915 May 19	♋	00°00' to 2°30'			

URANUS CONJUNCT NEPTUNE

1821 Dec 8	♑	00°00' to 2°30'	1993 Aug 19	♑	17°30' to 20°00'
1993 Feb 2	♑	17°30' to 20°00'	1993 Oct 25	♑	17°30' to 20°00'

URANUS CONJUNCT PLUTO

1851 Mar 19	♈	27°30' to 30°00'	1966 Apr 5	♍	15°00' to 17°30'
1965 Oct 9	♍	15°00' to 17°30'	1966 Jun 30	♍	15°00' to 17°30'

NEPTUNE CONJUNCT PLUTO

1892 Apr 25	♊	7°30' to 10°00'

APPENDIX I

The Composite Dwad-Wheel

This is the Natural Zodiacal Wheel. Its use in the analysis of any Chart, Natal, Mundane or Horary, adds a wealth of specifics and particulars.

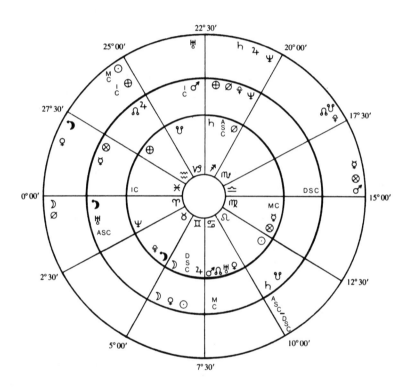

A ZODIAC WITHIN EACH SIGN,
A WHEEL WITHIN EACH HOUSE

Fig. 21. The Composite Dwad-Wheel

The innermost wheel: the Zodiacal Signs. (The sign ♈ is placed in House I of the Dwad Wheel.) The middle wheel: the Dwad-Sign Wheel. (Thus a Planet in a Dwad-Sign is related to the Zodiacal Sign of the same name.) The outer wheel: the Dwad-House Wheel. (Thus a Planet in a Dwad-House is related to the corresponding House in *any* Wheel.)

The above Composite Dwad-Wheel is for Bernard Baruch. It is oriented to Aries, i.e., Aries is placed in the first division (House) of the Wheel. Thus it is related to the Natural Zodiacal Wheel. The Natural Zodiacal Wheel refers to all of Nature and to Humanity, Man in a generic sense.

For "specifics and particulars" always make this Dwad-Wheel for any and every Chart you make. Do this for natural phenomena such as earthquakes etc.; for Celestial phenomena such as seasonal Ingresses, Eclipses, New Moons. Pay special attention to the Dwads occupied by the Sun, Earth and to Mars and Pluto, the co-rulers of Aries. Of course the Dwad occupied by a Stationary Planet or the conjunction of two Major Planets is outstandingly significant.

Make this Composite Dwad-Wheel of the Chart of an important event, personal or mundane. Make one for any Chart of the birth of a Question (Horary) as well as for the birth of a person. Do one for your pet if you have its time and date of birth; if you have only the date the Moon cannot be placed in a Dwad.

Remember the Natural Zodiacal Wheel relates to the world of minerals, plants and animals as well as to humans.

Leipert brought out that tendencies shown by this Wheel are not always on a conscious level. He related Mars to what some call the libido, psychic energy, which may express in sex, survival, etc.

An earnest student of Jungian Analytical Psychology, Leipert considered Pluto to be the major planetary component of the Collective Unconscious. True, he did not live long enough to accumulate a thousand Charts to offer conclusive proof of Pluto's co-rulership of Aries, but he "leaned heavily" in that direction. Pluto is the Planet of integration, completeness, wholeness, etc. Leipert suggested Pluto could well be called the Planet of the One Conscious.

Incidentally Pluto correlates to the higher sensory perception called telepathy. Leipert considered telepathy possible, not because of a communication between minds but telepathy is a contact within the One Consciousness.

Following a suggestion by Leipert, even without a Chart set up for any exact time, I notice the Dwad-Sign and Dwad-House occupied by Transiting Mars and Pluto as important "specifics and particulars" about what is going on currently. Of course the Dwad-Sign and Dwad-House of the Transiting Sun should always be considered.

The STAR WHEEL of Bernard Baruch

I have used capitalized letters in the word STAR to distinguish this from any actual Star in the sky. This seemed to be preferable to the enclosure of the name within quotation marks every time.

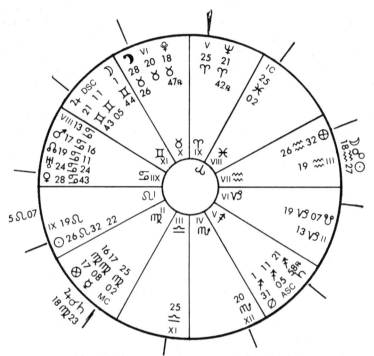

Radix Map (Fig. 17) is on page 53 with birth data.

Fig. 22. The Star Wheel for Bernard Baruch

The STAR WHEEL is made by the placement of the entire calculated Radix in the Solar Wheel. Then the Solar-Equilibrium Cusps are drawn like spokes in the Wheel. The glyph for Aries is drawn inside where 0° Aries appears in the Solar Wheel.

This is a Composite four-fold Nativity oriented to the Sun-Sign.

While the calculated Radix is a map of the Solar System in relation to the Earth, birthplace of the individual, at the center of the map. The Natal STAR WHEEL is a symbolic map of the individual's City of Consciousness. It is a map, so to speak, of the Psyche.

The Natural Zodiacal Wheel begins at 0° Aries, shows the natural tendencies, conscious and unconscious, of the individual.

The Solar-Equilibrium Wheel shows the focused awareness or conscious urges and will to be, have, etc.

The Solar Wheel shows the overall potentials of the individual, the capacities to be and to do.

The calculated Radix shows the physical body, environment and actual conditions, the attitudes and possible actions in the physical three dimensional world. It shows the possible interaction with others in the world and where such action and interaction take place.

Leipert researched the House Cusps of three systems — Placidian and those of Campanus and Regiomontanus, to see which Cusps were most correct according to the Dwads occupied in the respective systems. The Placidian Cusps were convincing; the others were not. He used Charts of Celestial phenomena as well as Charts of individuals to ensure accuracy of the Charts he used in this research. This is the reason I personally advocate Placidian Cusps and am still satisfied after so many years of their use.

Leipert did not deny, nor do I, the great significance of the calculated Radix Map. In fact, there is no substitute for it. To a person who lives on a purely physical level in the three-dimensional world, the Radix may seem most important of all the Natal Charts. To the individual who knows that "Consciousness is the great reality" the STAR WHEEL includes the physical phenomena within a broader and deeper context.

The New Moon before birth is written outside the Natal STAR WHEEL. The Full Moon before birth (if born in decreasing Moon period) is written outside also.

The Solar Eclipse prior to birth is written outside at the appropriate place. The New Moon before birth may be the Solar Eclipse as in Mr. Baruch's Chart.

You may note the degree and minute of the Sign as above; or you may designate the Dwad-Sign and Dwad-House occupied by the New Moon, perhaps the Full Moon, the Solar Eclipse and the Jupiter-Saturn conjunction previous to birth. After all, the purpose is to find the Dwad occupied by each of these Sensitive points. See Table 34 for Dwads of Solar Eclipses. See Table 36 for Dwads of Jupiter conjunct Saturn. Analyze these important Dwads in relation to your own life.

I write the Dwad occupied by the Natal Sun inside a large 'D', for Dwad, outside the Natal STAR WHEEL. Leipert called this Dwad the "Golden Door to the Self."

Supplementary Composite Dwad-Wheel

This is the Dwad-Wheel oriented to the Natal Sun-Sign. In other words, the Natal Sun-Sign is placed in House I, as in a Solar Chart.

Its use in the analysis of an individual's chart adds a wealth of specifics and particulars.

I use both Composite Dwad Wheels for an individual.

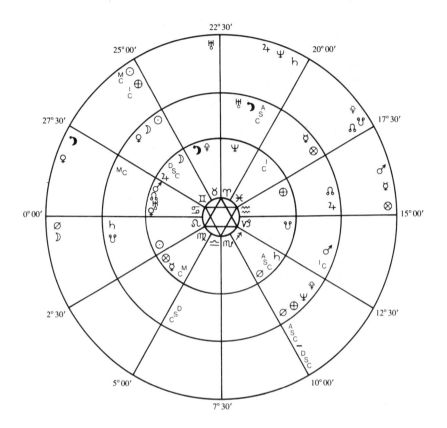

A ZODIAC WITHIN EACH SIGN,
A WHEEL WITHIN EACH HOUSE

Fig. 23. Supplementary Composite Dwad-Wheel

In the center is the symbol of the STAR. The innermost wheel: the Zodiacal Signs. (The Sun-Sign is placed in House I of Dwad-Wheel.) The middle wheel: the Dwad-Sign Wheel. (Thus a Planet in a Dwad-Sign is related to the Zodiacal Sign of same name.) The outer wheel: the Dwad-House Wheel. (Thus a Planet in a Dwad-House is related to the corresponding House in the STAR WHEEL or Solar Chart.)

When the Natal Sun is in Aries, the two Dwad-Wheels would be identical; no need to make a second one.

For the individual whose Natal Sun is in a Sign other than Aries, a second Dwad-Wheel can add many insights.

It's very easy to make this second Composite Dwad-Wheel for the individual.

The Supplementary Dwad-Wheel for Bernard Baruch

After you become thoroughly familiar with the Composite Dwad-Wheel oriented to Aries, I urge you to make this Supplementary Dwad-Wheel for each individual. It is highly effective in relation to business, corporations, institutions and government or whatever might be called an entity. I would not use this Supplementary Dwad-Wheel for an earthquake or a Horary question or a celestial phenomenon, etc. But for a marriage it could provide insights. Nevertheless, until you have used it for individuals only and gain experience in interpretation, I suggest you do not use it with other charts. Later you may experiment with it to advantage.

Please compare the two kinds of Composite Dwad-Wheels. See Figs. 21 and 23 in this Appendix.

The Planets occupy the same Signs but, unless the Sun is in Aries, in different Houses. The Dwad-House positions of the Planets are identical in the outermost circle. However, the Signs have shifted positions in the Wheel. At first, the making of this supplementary Composite Dwad-Wheel requires careful attention so that you place the Planets in the correct division of the Wheel. Double check to be sure of placements.

In the 11th Dwad-House, Baruch's Natal Sun shows the importance of hopes, wishes, associates, friends and circumstances themselves. Same in both Fig. 21 and Fig. 23.

In Fig. 21, the Dwad-Sign Gemini is in the 3rd division of the Natural Zodiac — mental pursuits, information, communication, verbal and otherwise. Now in Fig. 23 the Gemini Dwad-Sign has shifted to the 11th House counted from Leo, his Sun-Sign, to denote the counseling, advisory capacity, etc. This is just a clue for you to follow. You should elaborate on this Supplementary Dwad-Wheel when you analyze the Charts of individuals. May this material mean as much to you as it means to me.

An Easy Way to Find the Chaldean Rulers of the Decans

Since childhood I have continued to use my ten fingers as memory aids. At times my two feet are included to make the twelves often needed in Astrology. Of course this is a childish or primitive kind of counting and mental association. But, assuredly, the system works!

Place your hands in front of you with palms down, fingers outstretched and separated. Begin with the little finger of your left hand as we are "reading" from left to right. Beginning there with Aries, name each finger after the successive Signs. The little finger of your right hand will be named Capricorn. Then name your left foot Aquarius and the right foot Pisces.

Now, allocate each finger and each foot to the days of the week, starting with Tuesday, day of Mars.

Table 37
Table to Find Chaldean Rulers of the Decans

		Left hand			
Little finger	♈	Tuesday	♂,	☉,	♀
Ringer finger	♉	Wednesday	☿,	☽,	♄
Middle finger	♊	Thursday	♃,	♂,	☉
Index finger	♋	Friday	♀,	☿,	☽
Thumb	♌	Saturday	♄,	♃,	♂
		Right hand			
Thumb	♍	Sunday	☉,	♀,	☿
Index finger	♎	Monday	☽,	♄,	♃
Middle finger	♏	Tuesday	♂,	☉,	♀
Ring finger	♐	Wednesday	☿,	☽,	♄
Little finger	♑	Thursday	♃,	♂,	☉
		Feet			
Left foot	♒	Friday	♀,	☿,	☽
Right foot	♓	Saturday	♄,	♃,	♂

The Planet of the Day rules the first Decan of each Sign. The two Planets that follow rule the second and third Decans respectively. Note that these rulers are in the Chaldean Order, the reverse of the order of their speeds of motion. However, instead of beginning with Saturn, the slowest of the seven Planets of the ancients, begin with Mars, ruler of the first Decan of the Zodiac.

Using this simple method, you can find any Decan according to Chaldean rulership when there is no table available. And you do not need to memorize it!

APPENDIX II

The Dwads of the Dwads or Sub-Dwads

Frankly, you could ignore this material entirely, confining yourself to the 144 'Doors' of the Zodiac. I consider the 144 Duodenary Divisions to be an integral part of interpretation of Astrology.

However, if you would like to refine your interpretation still further you should welcome this additional division of each 2½° Dwad into twelfths. The Zodiac consists of 360° of Celestial Longitude. Each Sign consists of 30°. Each Dwad consists of 2° 30'. The Zodiac contains 144 Dwads.

Each Dwad (2° 30') contains 12 Sub-Dwads of 12' 30" each. Each Sign contains 144 Sub-Dwads. The Zodiac of 12 Signs contains 1728 Sub-Dwads.

Please do not be intimated by such a figure! The following wheels will facilitate your occasional use of them.

Leipert used these for the Natal Sun for additional insights. The Natal Earth occupies the Sub-Dwad directly opposite the Sub-Dwad of the Sun; so you need not look it up.

Example: The Sub-Dwad of Mr. Baruch's Natal Sun

His Natal Sun is 26° Leo 32' 22" in the Gemini Dwad-Sign of Leo. Refer to Fig. 24. Find the wheel for the 11th Dwad of any Sign.

26° 32' 22" is between 26° 27' 30" and 26° 40' 00". This is the 8th Sub-Dwad.

The 8th Sub-Dwad is the 8th Sub-Dwad-House of the Gemini Dwad-Sign. Which Sub-Dwad-Sign is the 8th from Gemini? While you look at the wheel for the 8th Sub-Dwad, mentally place Gemini at the center, then count around from Gemini in the 1st to the 8th division which (from Gemini) is Capricorn.

Capricorn is the Sub-Dwad-Sign of the Natal Sun, giving an ambitious, achieving, patriarchal, businesslike character and 8th Sub-Dwad-House connected with research, investigation and joining of efforts regarding mutual benefits and joint money or others' assets.

Regarding Figure 24

The Wheel for the 12 Sub-Dwads in the 1st Dwad shows the spaces occupied by each 12' 30".

The other Wheels in Fig. 24 continue with 12' 30" in each division (Sub-Dwad-House).

Look for the desired ° ' " of the Sun in the Wheel for the Sun's *Dwad* of any Sign.

The 1st Sub-Dwad-Sign always has the name of that Dwad-Sign.

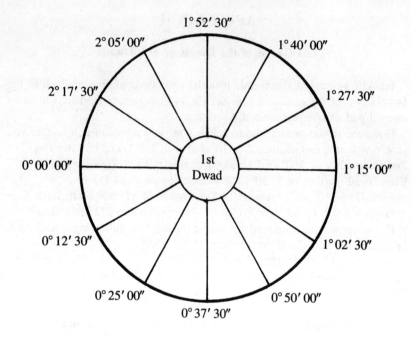

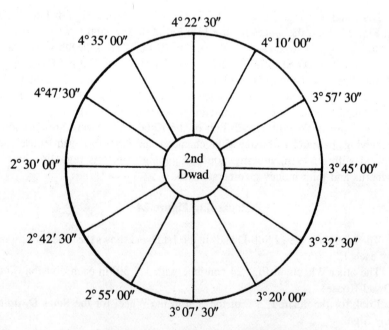

Fig. 24. Dwads of the Dwads, or Sub-Dwads

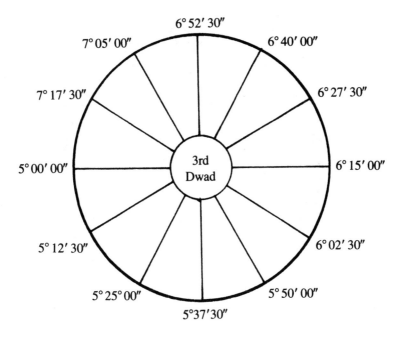

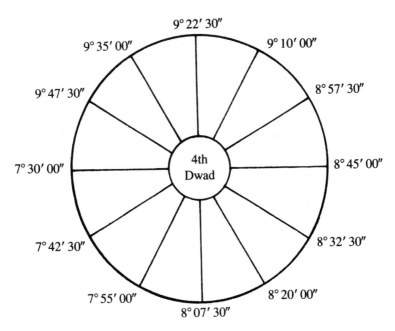

Fig. 24 — continued

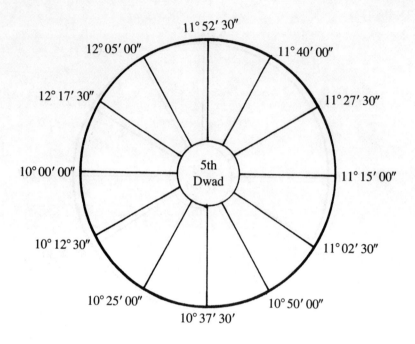

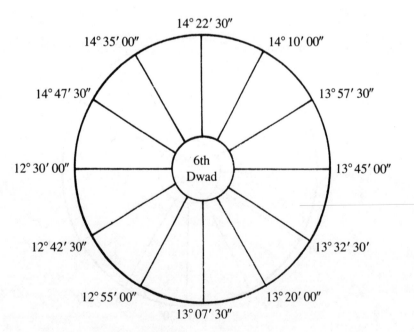

Fig. 24 — continued

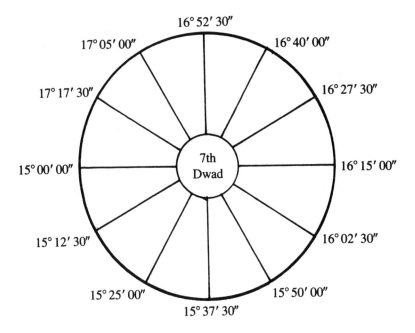

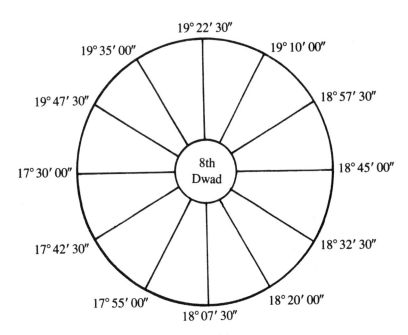

Fig. 24 — continued

104

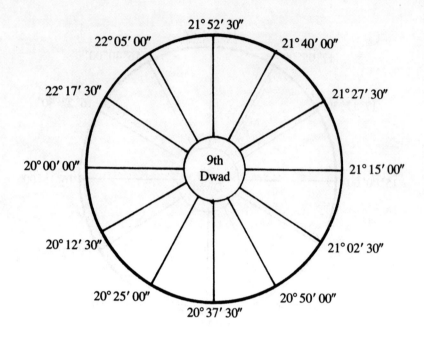

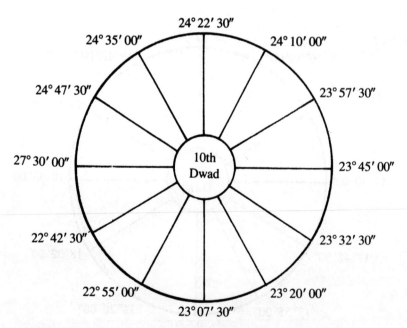

Fig. 24 — continued

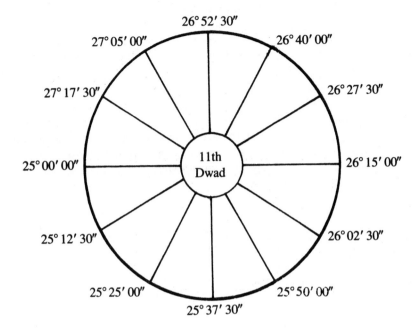

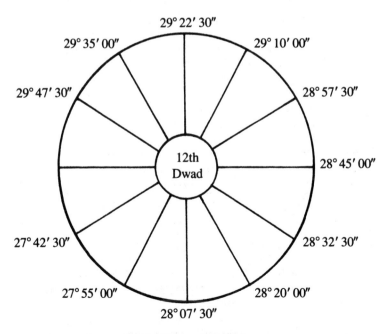

Fig. 24 — continued

Sub-Dwad of the Earth

All of this Sub-Dwad interpretation is only a highlight or accent in the interpretation of his Natal Sun in the Gemini Dwad-Sign, while in the 11th Dwad-House of the Sign Leo.

His Natal Earth at 26° Aquarius 32' 22" occupies the opposite Sub-Dwad-Sign, not Sub-Dwad-House, namely the Cancer Sub-Dwad which is the 8th Sub-Dwad-House of the Sagittarius Dwad, the 11th Dwad-House of the Sign Aquarius. Here we see a highlight or accent on an instinctive or basic feeling for and a tenacious holding on to (Cancer) mutual assets (8th Sub-Dwad-House) relative to expansion and future plans (Sagittarius) in regard to associates and important hopes (Aquarius Sign).

Leipert did not apply the Sub-Dwads to the Planets, True Nodes, Radix Angles or Arabian Parts. Nor did he use them in regard to Celestial Phenomena. He said that the placements of such were not precise enough.

Leipert did, however, use these highlights and accents for the Sun and Earth (which should be calculated to the second of longitude). He used them when doing certain Cycles and long periods which exceeded 144 years.

If interested in numerical symbology you might appreciate Leipert's remarks about the 144, number of Dwads and 1728, number of the Sub-Dwads. Leipert was, as mentioned, an earnest student of Qabalah which included the symbolic meanings of the letters of the Hebrew Alphabet with their numerical values.

144 reduced to a digit = 9. 1728 reduced to a digit = 9.

The numeral 9 is the inclusion of all digits, symbolically (a universal number). 9 can be added to itself over and over; it can be multiplied by itself and still reduce to the digit 9.

Are you interested in Qabalistic enumeration? If so, this is for you. According to the Qabalists 9 is the number of Truth. In Los Angeles, California, Leipert studied Qabalah with the Polish-born Rabbi, Maurice Abramson.

Through these studies Leipert told me the following regarding the 144 Doors:

Numerical value	Hebrew letter	Letter's meaning	Astro-correlation
100	Qoph	Back of head, a knot	Pisces
40	Mem	Water	Water (Ψ)
4	Daleth	Door	Venus

This is the mystery, the realm of the Unconscious, behind and within the tangible manifestations, where all is tied together in a universal way. The 100 is still the One with the 2 zeros of potential.

The 40 is the Element of Water, the Universal Solvent, the reflective and sustaining Element that is represented by Neptune. The "knot" ties it all together. Neptune (not known by the early Qabalists) represents Water and involves creative imagination, imagery and the intuitive activity of the Unconscious.

The 4 is the Door (the Door of Consciousness) the opening for the focus on specifics and particulars, correlates to Venus, Planet of refinement, finesse, finish, and fruit of experience. Venus is opulent, fruitful, pleasing and of value. Notice that Neptune is the modern co-ruler of Pisces while Venus is exalted in Pisces.

One reason why Leipert called the Dwads the "doors" was because of the Daleth — Door. The 144 also is related to the 144,000, the Elect, the Saved of biblical mention. Here again the digit 9 is universal.

Re the 1728 Sub-Dwads:

1,000	large Aleph	Ox, bull	Air (ꜧ)
700	final Nun	Fish	Scorpio
20	Kaph or Khaph	Palm of hand	Jupiter
8	Heth	Field or fence	Cancer

The large Aleph for 1,000 reduces to 1, Aleph, as a digit, the numeral for the Everliving One, Who Is, was and shall be. This is the Ox, Bull or Elephant of power. It correlates with the Element of Air, the Breath of Life, the animating Element, represented in modern times by Uranus, inspiration, electricity and vibration.

The 700 is the final form of Nun, the fish of productivity. Its final form shows augmentation. Nun is not Pisces, but Scorpio, transformation, transition, exchange and production.

The 20 is the Kaph or Khaph, the palm of the hand, the cupped hand that gives and receives, the mold to which the contents are shaped. Jupiter is the revealer, the extended, the abundance.

The 8 is the Heth, is the field to be cultivated and the hedge or fence that encloses. Cancer is the home base, the place to be cultivated, the termination as well as foundation. Cancer envelopes and holds.

So we shall go no farther into subdivisions of the Sub-Dwads!

The 9 as final digit of each set of divisions is letter Teth, which means Serpent or Roof and correlates with Leo. Serpent implies the eternal (Serpent with tail in mouth) of wisdom of the ages. The Roof implies a refuge of safety. Leo is creativity, self-expression, the drama of life, and the heart of the matter.

Of course, you did not need to know these items in order to interpret the Dwads and Sub-Dwads correctly and well. Nevertheless, to me it added something of value and I want to share it with you.

Also, for added information, Leipert was well versed in Tarot. He was acquainted with Paul Foster Case whom he greatly respected for his vast knowledge and thorough teaching of Tarot. Leipert used the same astrological correlation with the Tarot Keys that Paul Case gave.

Incidentally, Leipert, as well as Rabbi Abramson, gave to Pluto the representation of the Element of Fire, the letter Shin or Sin. The other Higher Octave Planets, Uranus and Neptune, represent the Elements of Air and Water respectively, as seen above.

In one of his excellent texts C.E.O. Carter gives some space to the Sub-Dwads. I am very sorry that I am not at the moment able to give the exact reference.

* * *

I personally think that the Sub-Dwad can be used for positions of Planets (even though they are calculated only to the nearest minute of longitude) *unless* they are so close to the borderline between Sub-Dwads that they might be placed in the wrong one. I think the True Nodes can be included as well, unless "borderline."

The Radix M.C. might be included. However, the Radix Ascendant should be excluded unless proportioned for exact Latitude and Sidereal Time. Furthermore, the time of birth must be exact.

Please, please do not be so carried away by the Sub-Dwads you grant them more importance than the Dwads and the Signs themselves.

Signs describe and characterize. Dwads show specifics and particulars.

Sub-Dwads provide highlights and accents.

109

ASTROLOGICAL BIBLIOGRAPHY

Beausar, W. Van Breda (C. Aquarius Libra). *Ephemeris of Lilith & Lulu*. Bandoeng, Java, 1934.

DeVore, Nicholas. *Encyclopedia of Astrology*. Philosophical Library. New York, 1947.

Escobar, Thyrza. *Essentials of Natal Interpretation with Study Guide*. A.F.A. Tempe, Arizona, 1982.

Escobar, Thyrza. *Side Lights of Astrology*. G.S.R.H. Hollywood, California, 1960.

Escobar, Thyrza. *The Star Wheel Technique*. G.S.R.H. Hollywood, California, 1978.

Leo, Alan. *Dictionary of Astrology* (Edited by Vivian Robson). L. N. Fowler & Co. London, 1929.

Manilius: The Five Books of. English translation. A.F.A.

Oppolzer. *Canon of Eclipses*. Dover Publications, 1962.

Raphael. *Astronomical Ephemeris & Almanac*. W. Foulsham & Co. Ltd. London, 1935.

Sepharial. *Dictionary of Astrology*. W. Foulsham & Co. Ltd. London, 1921.

Sepharial. *Science of Foreknowledge*. David McKay Co. Philadelphia.

Ephemerides

Barth, Otto Wilhelm. *Die Deutche Ephemerides*. Munchen, Germany.

Jones, J. Allen. *Lilith and Lulu*. G.S.R.H. Hollywood, California, 1974.

Jones, J. Allen. *True Nodes of Moon and Planets*. G.S.R.H. Hollywood, California, 1974.

MacCraig, Hugh. *Ephemeris of the Moon*. Macoy Publishing Co., New York, 1951.

Michelsen, Neil F. *The American Ephemeris*. Astro Computing Services. San Diego, California.